ST DAVIDS PENINSULA

Dewisland

Photographs & Text
Jacki Sime

D0551976

Maps, Clare Dunn

Pebbles Books

Published by :
Pebbles Books
St Davids
Pembrokeshire
SA62 6SP

© photographs: 1999 Jacki Sime
© text: 1999 Jacki Sime
© maps: 1999 Clare Dunn
© excerpts from: St Davids/Tŷ
   Ddewi by Waldo Williams
   Reprinted by kind permission
   of Gomer Press, Llandysul,
   Ceredigion
Book Design: Jacki Sime
Production Assistant: Kate Gillam
Layout: Philip Dauncey

ISBN 0 9536349 0 6

Acknowledgements

This book would not have been
possible without contributions
and support from: Tim Bugler and
Moyra Sime and the invaluable
assistance of Pete Faulkner, Philip
Dauncey, Kate Gillam, Hannah
Sime and Jinks Sime.

My thanks also to Wyn Evans,
James Nicholas, Ian Panton
Sid Howells, Bernie Stevens,
Mike Rogers, Paul Raggett,
Margi Bryant, Rod Penrose,
The Pembrokeshire Coast
National Park and to Terry John
and The Janus Group (York) for
making available their research
on the archaeology & history of
the area.
Also to David & Gail Lloyd, Fran,
Sue and Shonagh, and the many
friends for their unwavering
support.

To Toby & Caitie

Rams Nose (Title Page) Newgale (Above)
Front Cover: Whitesands, Cathedral, Coast near Penberi & Puffins (Insets)

Prologue

I was privileged to be born and brought up in St Davids; therefore I was delighted to be asked to write a short introduction to this guide, the 'St Davids Peninsula'. Whenever I think of St Davids and the surrounding area I am moved by the genius of the land. What is its secret? The genius eludes definition, but we may have a sense of understanding when we look at the variety of exciting images which abound here, and when use is made of these images to map out a world which enriches experience. The experiences expressed are related to place and are sometimes of a mystical nature. The Peninsula glows in a light which is transforming. This light has always fascinated me. It is reflected from the rocks and the sea and it continually transforms the land. As I write, I have before me a map of the Peninsula. I am fascinated by the rich array of Welsh place names in the area. Looking at the coastal path from Abereiddi to Pen Dinas Mawr, names such as Penmaen Mawr, Porthmelgan, Porthselau not only appeal to the ear, but they have an unfailing quality to excite the imagination. These names remind us of the relation between land and language reaching back to the Age of the Saints. The latter half of the century has seen an ebb in the future of the Welsh language. It is my sincere hope that this excellent guide will not only help the reader to discover the land anew but also to realise its genius and hence a noble heritage.

James Nicholas
Former Archdruid of Wales & National Chaired Bard

ST DAVIDS PENINSULA

Newgale • Abermawr • Abercastle • Trefin • Abereiddi

Porthclais • Porthlisgi • Ramsey Island • Porthstinian

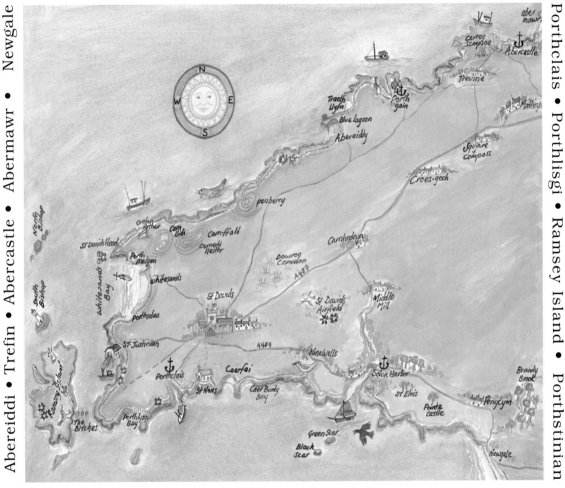

• Carn Llidi • St Davids Head • Porthmelgan • Whitesands• Porthselau •

Coast from St Elvis towards Ramsey Island

Contents

Introduction

Mesolithic hunters and Neolithic farmers;
Celtic monks and mediaeval pilgrims;
Viking raiders and Norman lords;
Modern tourists and visitors;
all these have made their way, in their turn
and in their generation, to this windswept peninsula
where the land juts out into the Atlantic.
This landscape, its hills and beaches has from very
remote times and for differing reasons, drawn human
beings to the far West.
Some, like David the patron saint of Wales, have come
here to be close to God in the sheltered valley
where St Davids Cathedral stands today.
Others, like William the Conqueror and countless others
since, have made pilgrimage to that sacred spot to which
two journeys counted as one to Rome;
others of his followers, more typically, pinned down the
country with a chain of fortresses. In our own day,
others come by their hundreds to the Pembrokshire
Coast National Park. They come to an area of
outstanding beauty where land and sea meet
together to form a unique landscape, blending
history, myth and legend.
It is my privilege to welcome this book which gives an
excellent foretaste of the delights of this county and I
foresee it being an indispensable guide in the hands of
all those who come to Pembrokeshire.

J. Wyn Evans
Dean of St Davids Cathedral

'A faint yearning comes to the sea strand.
Flood after flood calls out
amidst the stones' solidity.
Memory's speech is all yearning,
yearning for the land on the gravel and sand.
There is a long sleep in Pen y Fan, and through it
there is a yearning for the ocean in Porth Maelgan.'

Waldo Williams (1936)

Porthmelgan. Nr Whitesands (Above)

Rocks & Fossils

The particular characteristic of the St David's peninsula is a feeling of time, place and timelessness – a sense of connection to the past, present and an enduring future. This is nowhere more evident than in the rocks which form its backbone.

Shaped like a blunt-nosed triangle with its apex jutting into the Atlantic, the peninsula is bordered on both its northern and southern side by steep cliffs, inlets and sandy or pebble beached bays. Together with part of Ramsey Island, it is regarded as an extension of the 'Pembrokeshire Plateau' with its level plane broken by ridges of igneous rock. These outcrops, resistant to weathering and erosion, run from east to west, mainly along the northern section of the peninsula. The Ordovician intrusions of Carn Llidi and the sphinx-like Penberi are up to 120 metres (393 feet) higher than the plateau surface, overshadowing the smaller peaks of the Treginnis area. The Precambrian volcanic and intrusive rocks of this south-western promontory are some of the oldest rocks in Britain.

Along the southern coastline of the St David's peninsula, from Dinas Fawr to Porthclais, sedimentary rocks of the Cambrian age are exposed. It was within the middle Cambrian mudstones that the giant trilobite *Paradoxides davidis* was initially discovered in the 19th century. The fossil fauna of the *P. davidis Biozone* is interpreted as the first abundant trilobite community in south-west Wales consisting of more than 20 species of trilobite together with brachiopods and the primitive sponge, *Protospongia*. Good examples of specimens from this area are currently displayed at the National Museum and Gallery, Cardiff.

The cliffs at St Non's Bay and Caerfai Bay, are particularly colourful; rising from the basal conglomerates through the St Non's Sandstone and red Caerfai Bay shales to the Caerbwdi Sandstone. The Caerbwdi Sandstone is a famous purple building stone used in the construction of St Davids Cathedral. It was within the Caerfai Bay shales that the earliest Cambrian fossil remains were found. These remains included the brachiopod *Lingulella* and crustaceans, which indicated that this rock was formed from shallow water deposits.

On the northern side of the peninsula, between St Davids Head and Strumble Head almost vertical cliffs form an indented pattern, points of igneous rock alternate with inlets and small bays, eroded by softer sedimentary rock, or along faults. Mostly inaccessible except by sea, their boulder

The coastline from Penberi to the Ordovician intrusions of Carn Llidi (Above)

strewn beaches are havens for grey seals.

Abereiddi Bay, with its dark grey sand, is carved out of black Ordovician slate. This is well displayed in the sides of the quarry to the north of the bay. The deep 'Blue Lagoon' is the drowned lower level of the quarry workings. The slates at Abereiddi are renowned for their fossils of the 'tuning fork' graptolite *Didymograptus murchisoni*. It was from the vicinity of Llanvirn-y-frân Farm, Abereiddi, that the famous and controversial amateur geologist and medical practitioner, Doctor Henry Hicks (who originated from St Davids) first identified a distinct graptolite and trilobite fauna which was eventually to establish the Llanvirn Series of the Ordovician System in 1881. The wide valley behind Abereiddi Bay was formed by glacial meltwater and its now dry channel

links Abereiddi to Porthgain and separates Ynys Barry from the 'mainland'. The reasonably accessible west-facing bay at Traeth Llyfn is eroded into slates but its headlands are of igneous rock. Once thriving, the small ports of Porthgain and Abercastle stand at the seaward ends of valleys which penetrate the steep face of the cliffs. Abermawr and nearby Aberbach are fine examples of storm beaches, although not as impressive as Newgale which stretches for over two miles.

The Whitesands Bay area, as well as having one of the finest sandy beaches on the St David's peninsula, is also of particular interest to geologists as it presents rock types of Precambrian to Ordovician age. At Porthselau in the south, a succession of rocks from the Precambrian Ogofgolchfa group run through to the Cambrian sandstone of the Solva beds at

Point St John. In comparison the rocks that form the centre part of Whitesands Bay northwards to St David's Head display a progression from the Middle Cambrian mudstone of the *Paradoxides hicksii* Zone which pass into the Lingula flags of Trwynhwrddyn. The brachiopod *Lingulella* is of special significance as species of this group still survive today providing us with an example of longevity that has covered some 500 million years.

From Trwynhwrddyn passing northwards, the shallow water deposit of the Lingula Flags progress with unconformity into the Ordovician *Tetragraptus* shales of Porth Lleuog. These shales have been interpreted as a deep-water deposit containing the blind trinucleid trilobite *Bergamia*. North from Porth Lleuog, between the Ordovician igneous intrusions at Penlledwen headland and St David's Head lies Porthmelgan, excavated into the softer shales.

Ice sheets have passed over the St David's peninsula on more than one occasion and caused bevelling of the plateau edges. Evidence of the passing of the ice is provided by scratches on bare rock surfaces on the flanks of Carn Llidi and Penberi, and by

From Trwynhwrddyn to St. Davids Head (Above)

debris left behind as the ice sheets melted away. The ice sheets altered the drainage pattern of the peninsula. Both the rivers Alun and Solfach may have run into Whitesands Bay at one time before their channels became diverted southwards. When the ice sheets melted huge volumes of water flowed down these valleys.

The sea level has risen and fallen intermittently over long periods before becoming established as it is at present, covering stretches of former coastal plain in Cardigan Bay and St Brides Bay. When it rose at the end of the 'Ice Age', ten thousand years ago, the lower reaches of rivers were also flooded, creating drowned river valleys or rias. Examples can be seen at Solva Harbour and Porthclais in the south and the northern small ports of Porthgain and Abercastle. The stumps of ancient trees that grew on the coastal plains are occasionally exposed at very low tides in the sands at Newgale, Whitesands and Abermawr beaches.

Solva Harbour (Above)

A Glossary Of Geological Terms

- ❖ **Biozone:** A subdivision of rocks according to the biological remains they contain
- ❖ **Brachiopod**: A type of mollusc
- ❖ **Cambrian:** Very early geological period dated at 500-570 million years ago
- ❖ **Conglomerate:** Rock made up of pebbles or boulders in a matrix of minor material
- ❖ **Extrusive:** Rock resulting from molten lava on the ground surface
- ❖ **Fauna:** Animals of a particular region or period
- ❖ **Fossil:** Object found in strata of earth recognizable as remains of plant or animal of former geological period
- ❖ **Gabbro:** Intrusive igneous rock
- ❖ **Graptolite:** Extinct colonial animal, composed of a chitinous external skeleton
- ❖ **Igneous:** Rock made-up of solidified molten lava
- ❖ **Intrusive:** Rock forced while still molten into cavities in pre-existing rock
- ❖ **Meltwater:** Water from under or edge of melting glacier
- ❖ **Mudstone:** A sedimentary rock of mud grade particles
- ❖ **Ordovician:** Period lasting from about 500 million to 440 million years ago
- ❖ **Period:** Secondary division of the geological time scale
- ❖ **Precambrian:** Period lasting from 5,000 million to 570 million years ago
- ❖ **Sandstone:** Sedimentary rock mainly of compacted quartz grains
- ❖ **Sedimentary:** Rock made up of sediments laid down following erosion or transport after denudation.
- ❖ **Series:** A third division of the geological time scale
- ❖ **Shales:** A sedimentary soft rock resembling slate
- ❖ **Slate:** Fine grained metamorphic mudstone
- ❖ **Storm Beach:** Composed of rounded pebbles deposited by the sea with the largest nearest the land
- ❖ **Tetragraptus:** A type of graptolite
- ❖ **Trilobite:** Extinct marine arthropod resembling a woodlouse with a three-lobed body
- ❖ **Unconformity:** A break in the layering of sedimentary or metamorphic rock

Wildlife

'The tiny islands of the sea
are a silver web on its edge.
Long singing comes there
and the waves' dance on the fringes of the land'.

Waldo Williams (1936)

Land & Sea

Shaped by the forces of wind and tide, the peninsula is fragmented by rocky coves, inlets and sweeping beaches, all edged by steep and often precipitous cliffs. Here is a rugged timeless beauty, a treeless landscape where plant and animal have adapted to their surroundings. Warmed by the Gulf Stream, frosts are rare and spring arrives early when the cliffs teem with the first of the wild flowers. Divided fields bound by cloddiau-stone clad earth banks protecting against the force of the prevailing winds-sweep to the edge of the coastal footpath.

Offshore islands and mainland cliffs provide ideal habitats for nesting seabirds while the grey seal haunts inaccessible coves and caves to breed. Whales, dolphins and porpoises reside, or on summer passage, roam the sea. Headlands jutting into the Atlantic provide glimpses of these sea-born creatures and seabirds skimming the water's surface.

Conservation

The land prized for its aesthetic beauty, fauna, and flora is protected by a variety of statutory and non-statutory designations. St Davids Peninsula has 83km of Heritage Coast and the coastal area is designated as a Site of Special Scientific Interest (SSSI). The cliffs are of international importance and are a candidate for EC listing as a Special Area for Conservation (SAC).

The mainland coast and Ramsey Island are designated as a Special Protection Area (SPA) under the EC Wild Birds Directive. The coastline, protected by the Pembrokeshire Coast National Park (PCNP), has a long distance coastal footpath (186 miles) cited as the Pembrokeshire Coast Path National Trail. The National Trust (NT) has coastal, heathland and woodland sites. The Wildlife Trust, West Wales manages Dowrog Common and Ramsey Island is owned by the Royal Society for the Protection of Birds (RSPB).

Wild Flowers of Coast, Heath & Hedge

From March through to July, wild flowers appear in colourful succession. Spring squill, thrift, sea campion, pink campion, kidney vetch, the first to border the Coast Path, flourish in the salt laden winds. At St David's Head and on the lower slopes of Carn Llidi a combination of periodic burning and the grazing of wild ponies on the maritime heath provide a perfect habitat for pale heath violet and heath spotted orchid. At the cliffs' edge flowers merge into typical maritime rock fauna. There rock samphire and rarities such as wild chives and a sub-species of rock sea lavender thrive, and, synonymous with a moist clean atmosphere, a myriad of lichens pattern the rock surfaces. Butterflies emerge, common blue, dark green fritillary, graylings; and adders appear with the warmth of the sun. In the autumn, purple heather and western gorse spread in profusion across the heath, changing the landscape once again.

Wave at Whitesands (Previous Page)
Herring gull (Top Left), Chough (Top Right), Coast Path and Common Blue Butterfly (Above)

Inland the 'Pembrokeshire fen mosaic' lowland heath of Dowrog Common, Tretio common and Trefeiddan Moor supports native species such as the rare pale dog violet, wavy St John's wort, yellow centaury and three-lobed crowfoot. Meadowsweet, pond sedge, yellow iris, hemp-agrimony, purple-loosestrife, greater pond sedge, bogbean, marsh cinquefoil and bulrush also flourish. Fourteen species of dragonflies, scarce damselflies and the fritillary butterfly thrive on Dowrog Common.

Bordering small lanes which ramble to the coast, primrose, lesser celandine, pink campion, lesser stitchwort and foxgloves bloom. Gorse, hawthorn and blackthorn crown the hedge-banks.

Seabirds

On the western side of Ramsey Island, from March almost to the end of July, the high cliffs are dominated by breeding seabirds. Razorbills and guillemots crowd

along granite ledges, while the kittiwakes' mud and seaweed nests hang precariously on segmented rocky ledges. On the lower slopes of cliffs

oystercatchers and shags can frequently be seen, while the puffin has a small presence on North Bishop and Careg Rhoson where their burrows remain undisturbed by rats; these comical birds are often seen zipping along the surface of Ramsey Sound. Greater black-backed and lesser black-backed gulls

have colonies on Ynys Bery Island, off the southern end of Ramsey.

A small population of Manx shear-waters breeds in burrows on Ramsey and can sometimes be seen from headlands at first light during the summer months, as they return from the Bay of Biscay. Fifteen miles to the south-west is Grassholm Island, and here thirty thousand breeding pairs of gannets congregate from February. These magnificent birds often feed off Whitesands and St Davids Head. Fulmars with their dramatically straight wings nest on grassy cliff ledges around the coast and, along the shore, rock pipits flit among the rocks.

Birds of the Scrub & Heath

The rare chough with its distinctive call, red legs and curved red beak is a familiar sight. Nesting in holes and crevices along the cliffs and caves, the choughs depend on foraging for invertebrates along the cliff top grass-lands and maritime heaths. Ravens have vast twiggy nests around the coast and along the Coast Path stonechats perch high on gorse; wheatear, linnet and whitethroat are often seen while skylarks sing above the grasslands.

Trefeiddan Moor (Top Left), Puffin (Top Right),
Razorbill (Centre), Guillemot (Above Left), Kittiwakes on Cliff Ledges,

Near Shore & Offshore Habitats

Near shore habitats are places that are simultaneously sea and land. Of the many different coastal ecosystems the rocky shore is one of the most familiar, here amongst the boulders and rocks, barnacles, periwinkles, top shells and limpets flourish with rock pools of anemones, corals, sponges and bryozoans.

In offshore habitats nationally scarce marine benthic species survive such as the gold and scarlet coral, *Balanophyillia regia* at Ramsey Island and sponges *Thymosia guernei* off Abereiddi bay.

Birds of Prey

The Peregrine, the most awesome of our raptors, dive at incredible speed on their prey, capturing the victim in their sharp talons in mid air. Buzzards spiralling high on warm thermals, are often bombarded by members of the crow family. Kestrels hover along the slopes of the cliffs and sparrow-hawks, flying low, speed between hedge-banks along quiet lanes.

Birds of Inland Heaths

Damp heathlands provide habitats for the moorhen, coot, reedbunting, sedge and grasshopper warblers. On the Dowrog, hen harriers roost in winter and short-eared owls and merlin are regularly seen with wintering wildfowl including teal, wigeon, shoveller, snipe and Bewick's and Whooper swans.

Other Birds of Interest

By mid-April swallows arrive over the meadows and the distinctive call of whimbrels on passage rises in the air. Late on summer evenings tufted lapwing, with plaintive cry, fly in flocks and curlews hasten to roost on the islands. Little owl and barn owl swoop in feathered menace on small rodents scurrying beneath bracken and gorse.

During late summer and early autumn St Davids Head provides sightings of migrants, particularly during early mornings on a south-westerly breeze.

Whales, Dolphins & Porpoises

St George's Channel which lies some fifteen miles west of St Davids Head, is a corridor for a surprising variety of whales, dolphins and porpoises either passing as seasonal visitors or recorded as present throughout the year. Most frequently sighted cetaceans, are the common dolphin, Risso's dolphin and minke whale. Although they spend most of their time in St George's Channel and off the Small's Lighthouse, they maybe glimpsed from headlands or in tidal races during calm sea conditions. Rarities include the fin whale and occasional sightings of the northern bottle-nosed whale. Most near shore sightings are of bottle-nosed dolphins and harbour porpoise, with the latter sighted throughout the year around Ramsey

Notes:
Cetacean, is the collective word used to describe whales, dolphins & porpoises, derived from the Latin *cetus* (a large sea animal) & the Greek *ketus* (sea monster).
Fifteen species of cetaceans have been recorded in the area, five of which are frequently sighted.

Ynys Bery, off the southern end of Ramsey (Top Left), Rock Pool (Top Right).

Island, particularly between June and October.

Grey Seals

Pembrokeshire's grey seal population is estimated at about 5,000 individuals, which represents the largest population in Southern Britain. About 1,300 pups are born annually. The greatest concentration of grey seals is found on Ramsey Island with the highest number of mainland individuals between St Davids Head and Fishguard.

In late summer and early autumn the indented coastline, small inaccessible coves and caves and the offshore islands provide the ideal habitat for grey seals to gather and give birth. Adult females (cows), come ashore and have their pups above the tide-line. At birth, the pups weigh 14kg and are covered in thick folds of creamy-white fur which hangs loosely around their bodies. The cow bonds with her pup by identifying and distinguish-

ing its scent; once established a healthy pup suckles within the first few hours. The pups grow rapidly on the rich milk which contains 60% fat and 10% protein. With five to six feeds daily, each

lasting approximately ten minutes, the pup's weight will have doubled by the end of the first week. During this period the cows remain attentive to their pups and do not venture afield to feed. Consequently they lose about 4kg daily and eventually over one third of their original body weight of 170kg. Within eighteen days the pups weigh about 45kg and by twenty-one days they are weaned. Now barrel shaped in appearance with a thick layer of blubber, the pups remain ashore during the next seven days as they moult their white natal coat.

At about this time the cows become

sexually receptive and mate with the dominant male (bull) who appears when the first pups are born. Throughout this period, the bulls steadfastly patrol their territory. Between 200-350kg and at about two metres in length, the bulls are much larger than the cows; they also have a more pronounced 'Roman' nose and usually a darker less mottled coat than the females. The bulls, unwilling to leave their territory for fear of losing their position to a rival male at the breeding grounds also do not feed and lose approximately 2.2kg in weight daily.

After mating the cows leave the breeding grounds, the now fertilised egg undergoes a period of delayed implantation where it remains suspended for about 3 months. This enables cows to give birth at the same time each year.

The bulls remain until the last cow leaves. They may have mated with between two to ten females within their territory, although

Seals hauled out (Top), Newly moulted pup (Centre), Adult female-cow (Left).

some may have been mated by a rival male.

Meanwhile the now moulted pups are ready themselves to leave the breeding grounds and venture to sea to feed.

Sight, Diving and Feeding

Because seals' eyesight is perfectly adapted for low level light underwater, their vision on land is not as efficient and, although adequate, may suffer some distortion. Seals can, however, easily distinguish shape and movement and are quick to notice people on cliff tops silhouetted against the sky.

Seals are able to tolerate deep and long dives. Although they normally dive for around 5 minutes they can remain below the surface for up to 30 minutes. In order to achieve this and avoid the 'bends', seals breath out as they dive and carry the oxygen they require combined to special pigments in their blood and muscle tissue. At the same time their heart rate is reduced to around 40 beats a minute for shallow dives and between 4 to 5 beats for longer dives. Once they surface this races up to 120 beats a minute or more. In British waters it is thought that grey seals normally feed near the seabed in depths of around 50 metres.

Code of Conduct

Grey seal pups are very vulnerable particularly during autumn storms when they may be washed off the breeding grounds and may also become separated from their mothers.

If you find a seal pup on a mainland beach or are concerned about its welfare at some other location, please contact the RSPCA. Give your location, grid reference if possible, and any details about the condition of the seal. The more detailed your information the easier it will be to assess the situation. Do not approach the seal. Keep dogs at a distance. Any disturbance may cause unnecessary distress. Once alerted, the RSPCA will immediately contact a member of the seal rescue team who will attend to the seal.

Tel: RSPCA 08705-555999.

When to see Grey Seals & Identification

- ❖ During the breeding season Sept-Nov, peak October
- ❖ Bulls - larger than female weigh 200kg-350kg, 2 metres in length, 'Roman' nose, thicker necks, and generally darker coat
- ❖ Male average age: 20-25 years
- ❖ Cows - weigh 170kg, 180cm in length, flatter nose, generally mottled lighter coat, with 'pebbled' appearance
- ❖ Female Age: up to 35 years
- ❖ Pups - weigh 14kg at birth & are covered in creamy white fur
- ❖ Weaned by 21 days and weigh 45kg
- ❖ Moulting of natal coat begins at 21 days
- ❖ Adult coat is fully exposed by about 28 days

Adult male-bull (Top) Gannet flying past headland (Above)

Raiders

Invaders

Traders

&

Saints

'The blue spreads out towards Britanny-
The dark ridges are the land of the hermits,
the tight girths come from the rugged corners.
Here Samson of our brothers will be remembered.
And the old ways of the ocean open beautifully'.

Waldo Williams (1936)

Stand for a while before the waves at Whitesands. Half close your eyes. Let the sound of children playing fade into softer focus, and allow your mind to drift back through the centuries. This beach and others like it were the termini and freight depots of earlier civilisations. St Davids owes its success and importance down the millennia to this location, at the only intersection of the great north-south route along the west coast of Europe, and the east-west route out of the Bristol Channel to the south coast of Ireland. The human story of the St Davids peninsula begins here, some ten thousand years ago. For two thousand years, the weather in the west of Britain had been improving, eventually it became warm enough for groups of hunters to migrate from warmer, more southerly climes, in pursuit of great herds of horses and reindeer that roamed the tundra and steppe of the dying Ice Age. These were the original Stone Age Men.

The end of the Ice Age, officially put at around 8,000 BC, was in fact gradual. You would not have noticed the improvement if you had been around. The St Davids peninsula at this time must have been pristine, unmarked by man, bounded by low-lying, forested and marshy land extending seawards for some distance beyond the present coast.

Mesolithic Hunters
Slowly, however, the cold, dry conditions of the last phase of the Ice Age gave way to a warmer and wetter climate. A modern animal population, red deer, wild cattle and pig, began to replace the earlier one, and the human population started to leave their caves in favour of open settlement. This was the Mesolithic era, or Middle Stone Age.

Middle Stone Age people must have spent much of their time on beaches, looking for flint, their single most important commodity, washed ashore after falling out of the melting ice which had collected it, thousands of years earlier, during its advance across north-east Ireland. The precious raw material was taken back by the searchers to master craftsmen to be made into scrapers, borers, spear-points and arrow heads, the bow being used for hunting

for the first time during this period.

It was an exceedingly skilled process, and seems to have taken place at a few specific sites where collections of worked flints have been found. One of the most sizeable in West Wales, was at Nab's Head, on the southern shore of St Bride's Bay, where over 35,000 pieces of flint were discovered. A quantity of flint scatters have also been located at Clegyr Boia, just outside St Davids, suggesting a community there some 6,000 years ago.

Neolithic Farmers
About 5,000 years ago, a new way of life reached the peninsula. For hundreds of years, spreading from somewhere in the eastern Mediterranean, possibly originating from the Bible lands, came one of the greatest advances mankind has ever made: agriculture. The New Stone Age folk who brought it, short, dark-haired, and dark-eyed, were the first Welsh farmers. Clegyr Boia was certainly a settlement at this time. Excavations in 1943 revealed the pre-existence of oval and rectangular huts of wattle-and-daub. One of the huts consisted of two rows of posts, which possibly supported a wooden roof. Other huts had foundations of stone. A midden was discovered on the western side of the site, and from here, oak and birch charcoal, pottery and limpet shells have been retrieved. These collectively with cattle bones found on the floors of the huts indicate that the Neolithic people of Clegyr Boia, although still hunting and gathering, were now becoming dependent on agriculture for their food supplies.

There is little doubt that the descendants of these extraordinary people are still among us. However, they are remembered chiefly for the tombs they built for their dead, the prominent burial chambers, or cromlechau. Originally, a mound, or barrow of earth, would have covered the great capstone and supporting standing-stone pillars, possibly with the outer shell covered in pebbles. Within the tombs central chamber, the dead were laid to rest, knees drawn up in the foetal position, to await the new birth. Before interment they were probably placed

Coetan Arthur, Cromlech on St David's Head (Previous Page)

Before interment they were probably placed outside to become skeletonized. The chamber would then be opened, all previous burials removed, and a bone from each replaced with the new occupant to maintain continuity. The tombs were frequently finished with the mound curving round in a horn shape, creating a small forecourt before each cromlech, which may have been used for ceremonial dancing. Nobody knows for sure, but it is likely that burial in the great cromlechs were reserved for members of the higher echelons of society. Archaeological evidence suggests that the tombs were in use for many centuries.

The St Davids peninsula boasts two spectacular examples of such cromlechau, Coetan Arthur (Arthur's Quoit) at St Davids Head and Carreg Samson (Samson's Stone) at Longhouse, near Abercastle. The Longhouse capstone weighs twelve tonnes; that at Coetan Arthur is twelve feet long. Since the technology of Stone Age man was limited to wooden rollers and levers and perhaps grass ropes, it is worth reflecting on the incredible skill required to raise them on their pillars. Clearly these people were capable of remarkable feats of engineering.

Thousands of years later, people looking and marvelling imagined that the tombs must have been the work of giants, playing quoits with these massive stones. In addition to the cromlechs, smaller burial chambers were also built, possibly by family groups, by using existing materials and the shape of the land. Two such exist on the north-west side of Carn Llidi, above Whitesands Bay, formed by digging under large pre-existing boulders in the downward side of the hill, so that the capstone needed no raising and required support only at its raised end.

The Beaker Folk

The Bronze Age brought increasing levels of organization and sophistication to the peninsula. On Ramsey Island field boundaries, which perhaps date from this era, are still discernible. The population, called the Beaker Folk after their distinctive, highly decorated urns, began sailing for Ireland from Whitesands about 1500 BC, returning with copper from the Wicklow

Hills to be mixed with Cornish tin to make bronze. Later, gold mined in the Wicklow Hills was imported along a route which passed through Whitesands Bay and along the ridge of the Preseli Hills, the famous Golden Road, on the way to the centre of Bronze Age power at Stonehenge.

Bronze Age people were responsible for the erection of the enigmatic standing stones, or menhirs, positioned across the St Davids peninsula, they can mainly be seen within field boundaries or beside gateways. Their exact purpose is unclear. One popular theory is that they were used as stone computers, to calculate the passage of time and the passing of the seasons through the movements of the sun, moon and stars. Some stones may have been way-markers, and yet others may have been burial markers or the fairly obvious phallic foci of a fertility cult. What is known is that these

Cromlech, Carreg Samson (Above)

menhirs were once used as active ceremonial sites: across Wales, small pits have been unearthed beside menhirs filled with layers of charcoal, fragments of broken pottery, cremated bone and sealed with clay.

Particularly fine menhirs exist at Trecenny Farm, on the edge of the city, and on Dowrog Common, in the garden at the back of Drws Gobaith cottage. In the early 19th century, the Drws Gobaith stone was incorporated whole and undamaged into the wall of a ty-unnos, or moonlight house. An ancient law of settlement meant that a house built between dusk and dawn on common land gave the builder freehold tenure, provided there was a fire in the hearth and smoke coming from the chimney by day-break. The foundations of the ty-unnos still surround this stone. Two other good examples are at Tre-maenhir Farm, near Solva.

Irish Celts

The utilization of iron gradually extended throughout Britain from around 750 BC, although it appears to have been a rare and precious mineral during this period. Two schools of thought exist about the coming of the Iron Age; one is that the cultural changes that brought it came gradually, as a result of maturing developments in religion, technology and social structure. The other is of wholesale invasion. According to the latter, political pressures and a rising population in the centuries that culminated in Caesar's Gallic Wars began to force tribes outward from Central Europe. In Pembrokeshire's case, the theory is that a first wave came up the coast around 300 BC, and a second wave some 200 years later.

There was enormous pressure on agricultural land throughout this time, leading to friction between different tribal groups. Inland in England and Wales, this led to the building of hilltop forts, often large, with deep ditches and high earth-and-timber walls which meandered around the

apex enclosing them. The Pembrokeshire solution was to build similar fortifications across the narrow neck of a promontory. A number of these coastal forts (also called raths) are to be found along the St Davids peninsula. All are approached from the Coastal Path, at Caerau, Castell Coch and St Davids Head; Castell Heinif, Caerfai, Porth y Rhaw and the Gribin at Solva. Each carefully situated, the bank and ditch defences were far more formidable than now appears; eight feet or more of material must have slipped from the bank into the ditches in the two millennia since they were built.

The greatest of them all is undoubtedly that at St Davids Head, which has been described as an Iron Age treasure house, best seen in June before the bracken submerges so many outlines for another season. Here, dissecting the peninsula, the remains of a large dry stone wall, once fifteen foot high, can still be seen. Behind the wall, footings of six round stonewalled houses are clearly visible. Excavated in 1898, glass beads, spindle whorls, flints and pottery have been unearthed and are now displayed in Tenby Museum. The first Christian Fathers must have taught the message within its walls. Outside, between St David's Head and Carn Llidi, still visible are the remains of the field system used by the fort's inhabitants to grow their staples of emmer and spelt, peas, beans and barley. It is not known how long these forts remained inhabited, but some may have been

Stone Rampart - once 15ft high, St Davids Head (Top)
Remains of six stonewalled hut circles, St Davids Head (Above)

occupied, or re-occupied, as late as Viking times. In any case, it is worth stopping to consider that we are today still substantially nearer in time to these Iron Age folk than they were to the people who built the cromlechs.

Iron Age people had a profound belief in the power of the supernatural, wells and springs were seen as the entrances to the spiritual world. Legends associating wells, such as that at St Justinian, with severed heads and the power of healing probably date from this time, as may the enduring habit of throwing coins in a wishing well. Gifts were offered to ensure the goodwill of the gods, and the donation considered most favourable was a human head. Coins, bearing an image of a head, are a token substitute.

The Romans and the Demetae

The Romans arrived towards the end of the Iron Age, and there is a long-standing tradition that they built a fortification at Whitesands, which they called Menapia. No evidence of it has ever been discovered, though Roman coins have been found in the area. The closest acknowledged Roman settlement was at Carmarthen. The native Celts inhabiting the area at the time were a tribe called the Demetae. They do not seem to have particularly troubled the occupying power; consequently there is little information about them in Roman writings. However, the Romans undoubtedly knew of St Davids Head, the Roman geographer Ptolemy, born about 70 AD, named it Promontorium Ocupitarium, "the Promontory of the Eight Perils", almost certainly referring to the Bishop and Clerks, which are still a hazard to shipping.

The Romans never dominated the Atlantic zones in quite the same way as in lowland Britain, and when they withdrew in 410 AD they left behind a population well used to looking after itself. Therefore, while much of Britain relapsed into barbarism - the Dark Ages - Pembrokeshire by contrast emerged into an era of blazing moral sunshine known as the Age of the Saints, which was to last 400 years.

The Age of the Saints

No-one knows for certain when Christianity first arrived in Wales, but a great series of coastal missionary journeys had certainly begun by 450 AD. There is evidence that the St Davids peninsula may have been affected by two particular influxes of Christianity. Refugees from Gaul, escaping barbarism, expanded into Ireland and West Wales, bringing with them the Faith, and during the fourth and fifth centuries, immigrants from Ireland, many of them Christian, began arriving in north Pembrokeshire. We know of both groups from a series of inscribed stones. In the ancient church of Llanhowell, between St Davids and Croesgoch, is a pillar stone engraved with the words RINACI NOMENA, "the remains of Rinacus". It is not known who Rinacus was, but the inscription, dating to the fifth or sixth century, is similar to the examples from Italy and Gaul.

There are several so-called "Ogham stones", recording the names of the dead followed by an epitaph in both Latin and Ogham (an alphabet which appears to have been invented in Ireland, consisting of groups of lines or notches set out across a medial line). Ogham stones therefore mark

Whitesands (Above).

the arrival of Irish people into the peninsula, and a fine example (the Vendognus stone) exists in the church porch at Brawdy.

The Celtic Church was dependent upon the sea for nearly all communication, and as already noted St Davids stood at a great crossroads of long distance sea routes. It

was a time when men and women of great fortitude and resolve left their homes in Wales, Ireland, Scotland, Cornwall and Brittany to spread their beliefs, they travelled the length of the Atlantic coasts in their flimsy curraghs, a wooden frame of a boat, covered with skins. Eventually, many of these early missionaries elected to withdraw to places of isolation where they might worship God undisturbed. All around the peninsula memories of these people and their journeys survive in place, name and legend - St Justinian, St Elvis, and St David, to name but three.

King Arthur, History & Legends

King Arthur of Round Table fame has a pivotal role in the folk history of this period, figuring in the Mabinogion, a collection of Welsh folk tales which although first recorded in 1300 AD probably date back to the end of the Iron Age. One of the best known sagas of the Mabinogion is the story of Culwch, a nephew of King Arthur, who falls in love with the daughter of a giant. His prospective father-in-law grants Culwch permission to marry his daughter only on condition that he carries out a series of Herculean tasks. One of his labours was to find the Twrch Trwyth, a giant boar resident in Ireland, and recover a golden comb, scissors and razor that for some reason it carried between its ears. Accompanied by Arthur and many of his fearless warriors, Culwch pursued the boar across the Emerald Isle before the creature leapt into the sea and swam eastwards, finally coming ashore at Porthclais, followed by Culwch and his companions. The chase then proceeded north to Nevern and south again into the Preseli Hills before Culwch was able to grab the golden grooming kit and marry Olwen, the giant's daughter.

In considering this tale and the later journeys of the saints, it should be remembered that the Irish Sea was not nearly so wide then as it is today. In the second branch of the Mabinogi, "Branwen, Daughter of Llyr", it is made clear that in the very early days Wales and Ireland were separated only by two rivers. Certainly the sea overwhelmed the low-lying lands of Cardigan Bay in the 6th century AD.

In the period between the birth of Christ and the Norman Conquest (1066 and all that), it is hard to separate history from legend. In fact the lines between folk-history and folklore are often impossibly indistinct. There was indeed a real King Arthur, who is credited by the 18th century historian and cartographer Thomas Kitchin with having founded the Bishopric of St Davids in 519, when Saint David himself had reached the important mystical age of 77. Arthur apparently ruled the ancient kingdom of Dyfed until the age of 90, when he was beheaded after losing a battle near St Davids. The site of his execution is commemorated in the name of a farm on the road to Whitesands, Pen Arthur or "Arthur's Head".

It is said that the patron saint's birth was prophesied both by Merlin, King Arthur's

Towards Point St John (Above)

legendary magician, and by St Patrick, who had wanted to found a monastery in St Davids himself, but was warned off by an angel who told him the place was reserved. Patrick was then shown a vision of Ireland, and persuaded that was where his career lay. On at least one of his journeys across the Irish Sea he set sail from Whitesands, and a sixth century sailor's chapel, St Patrick's Chapel, marks the spot.

According to Geoffrey of Monmouth's version of the Arthurian legend, Merlin prophisied "A preacher of Ireland shall be dumb on account of an infant growing in the womb". This is supposed to have foretold an incident during which St David's mother, St Non, took shelter in a church where St Elvis was preaching. St Elvis found himself unable to continue with his sermon while the pregnant Non

remained because, according to protocol, he was not allowed to preach before the greater saint.

Much of what we know of St David comes from his "Life" written by Rhygyfarch, son of Bishop Sulien of St Davids, circa 1090, though there are as many descriptions of his birth as there are writers who recount it. One version, in verse, has even been attributed to Richard Coeur de Lion. Rhygyfarch's is probably the most accurate, and he claims to have sourced his work from very ancient documents preserved in the diocese. However, there seems little doubt that his intention was to create a work of propaganda to defend the Celtic Church against unwelcome encroachments by Canterbury.

The act of David's conception is often described as rape, although whether this was on account of the evidence or to avoid maligning the innocence of Non, will now never be known. According to the legend, David's father, Sant, Prince of Ceredigion, was out hunting when he came upon the beautiful Non, niece of King Arthur according to medieval genealogies. Overcome by desire he raped Non.

The resulting pregnancy went down badly with Non's father, a local chieftain named Cynir who plotted to kill his daughter and her unborn child compelling Non to flee. As the moment of birth approached, Non struggled through thunder, lightening, rain and hail, finally taking shelter under a ruined cromlech. "Then," says Rhygyfarch, "the place shone with so serene a light that it glistened as though the sun was visible, and God had brought it in front of the clouds." He goes on to tell how, in the pain of labour, Non grasped one of the standing stones so firmly that it took on the imprints of her fingers, and split in two, one part remaining behind her head and the other standing upright by her feet. As David was born, a spring of pure water gushed from the ground, and still remains, now known as St Non's Well, which is credited with powers of healing. The story of St David's birth fits neatly with the pagan Celtic belief that interference with any standing stone or cromlech brought on elemental disturbance. Non is said to have retired to Finisterre, Brittany, after the Saint's birth, and until

St Nons (Above Left), St Nons Well (Above Right).

the French Revolution a mystery play was acted annually in her honour, graphically re-enacting her story.

David The Water Drinker

'He comes from his charge as he came
to the sound of his hermit's life,
The tall man beloved by wave
and cliff above the ocean.
And the fervent waves break on the dunes,
and their voices whisper below once more.
'It is David they say, and their lips are so tender
about the name which they love'

Waldo Williams (1936)

About the only thing known with any certainty about St David the man is his asceticism. He was known as Dewi Ddyfrwr (David the Water Drinker). In this respect it can be said that David came in a direct theological line from the desert preachers of the Holy Land, John the Baptist, and indeed Christ himself.

St David was not nearly as austere as his friend and soul-mate St Justinian, however, who according to legend hacked off a portion of the St Davids Peninsula with an axe to create a true believers' paradise which we now call Ramsey Island and the remaining splinters, the Bitches. Little good that did him, though, for his followers on the island got so fed up with his extremism that they chopped off his head. Thereupon, the decapitated saint walked off across the water with his head tucked under his arm, laying it down when he reached the mainland at a point we now know as the holy well of St Justinian, near St Davids Lifeboat Station.

From what we know of the Iron Age cult of head worship, it seems reasonable to suppose that Justinian was in fact sacrificed to the Pagan gods. St Justinian's remains were buried at the site of a Celtic oratory near the well before being taken into the cathedral and re-interred with his beloved St David. Baptised by his cousin St Elvis, the Bishop of Munster, the young David was educated from childhood in the life of the Church. Rhygyfarch says he was told by an angel to build in the valley where the cathedral now stands, to the annoyance of a great local pagan, Boia, an Irish warlord and

a druid of some repute.

According to local legend Boia looked down from his fortified settlement on Clegyr Boia and saw smoke rising from the valley below. This was a ritual way of staking a claim, and the fire had been lit by David's monks. Boia sent his followers to drive out the saint, but they were defeated by a spell causing his people and livestock to collapse in apparent death. At this Boia gave in, became a Christian, and negotiated the lifting of the spell.

The feud was taken up again by Boia's wife (local tradition insists her name was Satrapa, although this is disputed by scholars). She began by sending young

women from her camp to romp naked in the river near David's encampment in a bid to lure his followers away from the life of self-denial with promises of something more exciting. When this failed, Satrapa resorted to human sacrifice, cutting her step-daughter Dunod's throat. What makes this bloody interlude particulary interesting is the ambiguity of Satrapa's action; human sacrifice was by now used only in extreme circumstances, such as serious territorial dispute, although, ironically it was also known to be carried out at the foundation of important buildings.

Most probably Satrapa intended to invoke the gods to destroy David's embryonic church, but just possibly she, too, was by then feeling "if you can't beat 'em, join 'em" and misguidedly thought that the sacrifice would be an appropriate demonstration of her change of heart. Either way, it had an

From the top of Clegyr Boia looking towards St Davids (Above)

electrifying effect. Satrapa became demented and the heart-broken Boia, neglecting his defences, was captured and beheaded by an Irish pirate, Lysgi, who stormed his camp. All resistance to David was defeated.

The First Foundations

No cathedral settlement in Britain has a longer continuous story: for more than fourteen centuries, for three-quarters of the history of the Faith itself, there has been a Christian community here in the valley which David won from Boia at the most western tip of Wales.

David's first monastery would have been basic, a fence surrounding roundhouses, a simple oratory and pulpit crosses. A succession of churches were built later following sporadic sackings by Viking invaders. The first solid Norman church was erected in 1131 by Bishop Bernard. David is credited with many miracles; the restoration of sight, the healing of the sick, and even the raising of a dead child.

The crowning moment of his career, and the one that effectively made him the archbishop of Wales, came in 545 at the so-called Synod of Brefi. At Llandewi Brefi in Cardiganshire, a meeting of clergy was called to discuss Pelagianism, a heresy which denied the doctrine of Original Sin. David was brought to the meeting and demolished the heresy with the sheer force of his argument. As he did so, the earth under him rose to form a mound, and a white dove, the symbol of the Holy Spirit down the ages, settled on his shoulder.

David is said to have attained the remarkable age of 147. According to Rhygyfarch, an angel of the Lord announced his impending death to his disciples in all parts of Great Britain and Ireland, that they might flock "like bees on a storm" to receive his last blessing. On Tuesday, March 1st 589, at the crowing of the cock, the valley by the Alun river was filled with the sweetest fragrance and the sound of angelic choirs singing celestial songs. Jesus himself appeared, David said to Him, "Lord, take me with Thee", and, accompanied by the angelic host, he departed to heaven. His last words to his followers were "do the little things that you have heard and seen through me".

Rhygyfarch says the air was then filled with the weeping and wailing of the people.

St David was buried in the graveyard of his own monastery. Centuries later, in 1275, the relics believed to be those of St David were disinterred and placed in the Cathedral where they remain, despite a discreditable later effort to disturb them.

Among the many age-old legends centring on the saint is the belief that at the special prayer of St David himself, Pembrokeshire people are endowed with second sight in order that they might bear witness to the existence of the spiritual world to future ages.

Viking Raiders & Norman Lords

Between the eighth and tenth centuries St Davids suffered much at the hands of Norse pirates, two bishops were killed in Viking raids and the settlement and its monastery were sacked in 1073, 1080 and 1091.

William the Conqueror visited St Davids in 1081. Apparently disguised as a pilgrim, he travelled through Rhodiad y Brenin on route, giving the village its name, Road of the King.

In 1115, Wilfred, the last of the Welsh bishops of St Davids, died, and the Normans secured the election to the episcopate of Bishop Bernard. Bernard's achievements were considerable. He erected, as aforementioned, the first proper cathedral (it was demolished after less than fifty years when a new building was begun by Bishop Peter de Leia, some of which remains as the oldest part of the present structure). He also established and organized a proper community of the Cathedral, with a chapter of canons and defined archdeaconries, which lasted for the next 800 years.

Giraldus Cambrensis (Gerald the Welshman) tried and failed to become Bishop of St Davids around this time. He was of Norman descent, but his mother was Welsh and he had little time for Norman ways with church property. He was a champion of the Celtic church, spending much time and energy as canon and archdeacon in trying to maintain St Davids' independence from Canterbury. He is best known as a superb chronicler; his books "The Itinerary through Wales" and "Description of Wales" are still in print.

It is generally accepted that David was canonized by about 1120, although there is no evidence that this was ever a formal event. Pope Callixtus II (1119-24), who is sometimes credited with the canonization, was certainly aware of, and approved of, the age-old veneration of St David. The tradition that "two pilgrimages to St Davids are equal to a pilgrimage to Rome" also started about this time.

Nearly three centuries later, in 1398, Archbishop Arundel ordered that the Festival of St David should be kept annually on the anniversary of David's death, and the Welsh have done so ever since-even during the Cromwell era, when there was a ban on saints' days. In fact St David is the only saint in the British Isles to have been born in the country which now reveres him as its patron.

The Black Book
The Bishop's Palace in its present form is the work of one of the greatest of medieval builders in Wales, Bishop Henry de Gower (1328 to 1347).

A double set of apartments enclose a central courtyard. Those on the eastern side were for the bishop, while the others were to be used for distinguished guests. By this time, St Davids had also become the centre of the great Marcher lordships of Wales (only one now remains, in Newport, Pembrokeshire) and it is likely that the great

hall of the palace was used for meetings and administering justice.

In 1326, 'The Black Book' of St Davids, an inventory of all the lands held by the bishopric, was drawn up on the orders of Bishop David Martyn. 'The Black Book' portrays an exceptional account of the town and outlying area. One hundred and forty mostly English burgesses, held burgages amongst the population of about one thousand which existed in St Davids at that time. These burgages were wholly or partly from the Bishop and service was also paid to the Lord Marcher. Rents were not just monetary. The Black Book records payments-in-kind of capons, gloves, wax and needles, which may have been used for repairs.

In 1536, William Barlow became the first post-Reformation Bishop of St Davids. He was a protégé of Anne Boleyn, a violent Protestant and most unpopular. He did his utmost to get the see moved to Carmarthenshire, and it is said that only the fact that Henry VIII's grandfather's tomb had been removed to St Davids at the Dissolution of the Grey Friars at Carmarthen, the king refused his request. Henry VIII did not interfere, however, when Barlow moved his Episcopal palace to Carmarthen, and sought to make the Bishop's Palace at St Davids uninhabitable by stripping the lead from the roof to provide dowries for each of his five daughters. The strategy paid off only partly; four of the Barlow girls married bishops, but the fifth was killed by a piece of lead hurled from the roof when she went to check on the progress of the operation. Her ghost haunts the ruins to this day. Barlow was aware of St Davids' reputation as a place of pilgrimage, but regarded it with scorn.

For the rest of the 16th century, Barlow's successors dwelt in habitable parts of the Bishop's Palace during their visits to St Davids. The last recorded use of the building by a bishop was in 1633, when a Chapter meeting was held there by Bishop Field.

The Cathedral also suffered during the Civil War. Cromwell is said to have ridden his horse into the building, leaving marks on the paving that can still be seen. A Puritan officer, Colonel Horton, ordered Parliamentary soldiers to strip more than thirty

Bishop's Palace (Above)

hundredweight of lead from buildings within the Cathedral Close thus causing considerable damage.

One of the best known of 16th to 17th century madrigal writers, Thomas Tomkins, was born in St Davids around this time. The grandson of a cathedral choirmaster, he came from a prodigiously musical family. No less than twelve Tomkins are mentioned in detail in Grove's "Dictionary of Music and Musicians". His masterpiece is probably the five part "When David Heard", and although he composed ten books of services and anthems, Tomkins was one of those who was deprived of their livelihood when music was forbidden in church during the period of Cromwell's republican government, the Commonwealth (1649 to 1660).

Land & Wealth
During the Reformation, much of the land owned by the Bishops of St Davids was sold to, or otherwise acquired, by the landed gentry. Businessmen took over the revenues of the Church and by the beginning of the 18th century two hundred and fifty parishes out of three hundred in the diocese were in the care of lay people and landowners. This led to a huge increase in the wealth of the Pembrokeshire squirearchy, and George Owen in his "Description of Pembrokeshire" (1603) said "I have not seen better or finer land nor greater store of corn than I have seen growing about St Davids." During the Hanoverian period, the Welsh cathedrals became increasingly derelict, and St Davids did not really find a champion until Connop Thirlwall, an Englishman who could speak Welsh, was appointed in 1840. He commissioned Sir Gilbert Scott to oversee a fifteen-year programme of restoration and reparation, saving the Cathedral from falling to ruins. Scott, responsible for the restoration of no fewer than half the cathedrals in England and Wales, rightly regarded his work at St Davids as one of his greatest achievements. He based his designs on an engraving of the 12th century structure, and in general he managed to tame his excessive zeal for tidying up the work of mediaeval architects.

The Dewisland population during the 16th and 17th centuries was fairly small, some of the larger farmhouses still lived in today date back in part at least to these centuries. Their most interesting features are the large rectangular chimneys, which project out from the main building and taper into a cone, known locally as Flemish chimneys or "Shimlau Fawr". Fine examples include Rhosson-Uhaf on the road to St Justinian and Hendre-Einon near Rhodiad-y-Brenin. The wattle and daub earthen floored homes of the peasantry have not survived.

The New Pilgrims
The history of the St David's Peninsula over the next two centuries was fairly uneventful, the most notable drama occurring in 1797, when the French landed at Fishguard to mount their unsuccessful and short lived "last invasion of Britain". St Davids itself was not endangered, but in the frenzy to repel the invaders, the local inhabitants threatened to take the Cathedral and so demanded that the lead be taken from the roof which was then divided up among six local blacksmiths and bullets produced; a mob marched towards Fishguard and the French surrendered after three days.

The early 19th century was a boom time. Farming thrived, large town houses were built. Restoration of the Cathedral began, trade through Solva and Porthclais prospered and the slate industry at Abereiddi was established. Employment was high.

Carriers and the Mail coach to and from Haverfordwest complained of the old road. A new one was built in 1840 through Solva but there were still '16 miles and 16 hills' to travel and passengers were obliged to walk up the hills to save the horses.

The sea having played a vital role in shaping the history of the peninsula, transporting passengers and cargoes, had become important as a trading route, Porthclais, Solva and Abercastle became active shipping ports. The earliest record of sea trade, was in 1385 when limestone, lead, iron and coal were brought ashore. Later, between 1550-1603 grain was exported and ships returned with wine, hops, raisins, calico, pepper and salt. During the 17th century 30 ships of 20 to 250 tons were owned and registered in Solva Harbour. Then mechanization struck. The railway arrived in Haverfordwest in 1854. Farm machinery and transport were run by steam engines. It became cheaper to carry goods by road and maritime trade ceased abruptly.

After 1860 the population fell. The labour force decreased. Young men left to work in the coalfields of South Wales and whole families emigrated. Large estates such as Trevacoon were sold piecemeal. Better slates produced in Caernarfon forced Abereiddi quarry to close in 1904. Porthgain too, once a hive of activity producing slate, brick and crushed roadstone for export ceased in the 1930s. Other small quarries up and down the coast were forced to close. Mills became uneconomic to run and there was a period of depression.

Not for long. Encouraged by easier access visitors and tourism increased. Mills and stately houses are now hotels; craftsmens' workplaces have become shops, art galleries and restaurants. Tourist centres have evolved, providing for environmental and historical interests and a wide range of outdoor sports. In 1952, in recognition of its outstanding landscape and heritage the Pembrokeshire Coast National Park was established.

Visitors come, new pilgrims, to roam a magnificent coastline, marvel at ancient history and contribute to the future.

Mad Point, between St Nons and Porthclais (Above)

The Cathedral

St David's Cathedral was built in honour of a man of profound influence who founded a monastery on the same site five hundred years earlier. In the 6th century, David (Dewi), brought a new ascetic discipline to an already established Christian belief among the Celts. He settled with his followers in the tranquil valley of the little river Alun to teach and to practice his way of life. After his death several successive churches containing his shrine were built and later destroyed.

Throughout the Middle Ages two pilgrimages to St Davids counted as one to Rome or three as one to Jerusalem and thousands flocked in penitence and homage to Tŷ Ddewi the 'House of David'.

It was not until 1181 that the Normans, the ruling power of that time, recognizing the importance of David, began their building of a more permanent structure that was to take hundreds of years to complete. The architecture and style of the Cathedral, although appearing as an unified whole, has been added to, redesigned and extensively repaired and restored throughout many centuries.

Invisible on the skyline, hidden deep and sheltered, stands the Cathedral Church of St David, ancient yet benign, and the graceful lichen-covered ruins of the Bishop's Palace. Dramatically revealed from above at the top of the thirty-nine steps below Porth y Twr, the Cathedral's buttressed walls of purple Cambrian sandstone from nearby Caerbwdi, leaded roof and square central tower combine in a building of impressive solidity.

Outside, the Cathedral is substantial rather than elegant. Situated on marshy land, eroded by underground springs and rocked by a minor earthquake in 1247, the building tilts downwards from east to west and is massively braced by great stone buttresses. Facing the Bishop's Palace the west front, with its heavy oak door, suffers constant damage from weathering and former subsidence. By the 16th century it had moved three feet out of the perpendicular. Attempts to repair it had been made, but it was not until the 19th century under George Gilbert Scott that its

St David's Cathedral looking down the valley (Above)

33

base was secured and the façade restored in a Gothic style. To the north of the Cathedral are the remains of cloisters and the Cathedral Hall, recently restored from the ruined chapel of St Mary College founded in 1365 to accommodate church dignitaries. The central tower, rebuilt in stages after collapse and later distortion of its foundations, no longer carries the weight of the bells that were removed to Porth y Twr above the valley. A 14th century porch protects the South Door into the Cathedral. Breathtakingly splendid, suffused with radiant light pouring through plain and stained glass windows, the interior of the Cathedral is enriched with the work of past craftsmen. Soaring high above the Nave a magnificent 15th century oak ceiling is decorated with intricately carved arches and pendants while on columns, screens and traceries the delicacy of the mason's skill is manifest.

The Cathedral is cruciform in shape with the longer arm of the cross running from west to east and containing the Nave, Choir (under the tower), Presbytery, Holy Trinity Chapel and the Lady Chapel in that order. The North Transept and St Thomas Chapel are on one short arm and the South Transept and Vestry on the other. Aisles run on either side of the central chapels.

The Nave
The Nave, with its aisles, is probably the oldest part of the Cathedral and was once used for processions. To the left of the West Door is a stone font where generations of babies have been baptised, for this is not only a cathedral, the setting for great occasions, but is also the parish church of St Davids, serving the needs of the community. An original bell and several inscribed stones rest near the font.

The floor of the Nave slopes upward from the west and the arcade columns lean outward, especially on the northern side, showing how the original foundations were inadequate to support the building. In the 15th century the roof of the Nave was altered in order to reduce weight and a false ceiling suspended from tie beams. This is the wonderful oak roof, already described. Over each aisle runs a gallery or triforium.

Dividing the Nave from the Choir is a gloriously ornate stone rood screen. Built by Bishop Gower in the 14th century to replace an earlier screen it is deep enough to

St David's Cathedral (Above)

contain his tomb. Above the screen are the hanging rood and a 20th century loft housing the great Willis organ.

A few steps up from the Nave is the North Transept containing the Chapel of St Andrew, leading into the Chapel of Thomas à Becket with its 14th century vaulted ceiling. The stained glass window and altar are 20th century and to the right is an ancient double piscina or hand-washing basin. Set aside for silence and prayer a lamp burns in the chapel denoting that consecrated bread is available for private Communion.

Above this chapel is the Library, reached by a winding and rather difficult stone stairway.

The Choir

Rich with the glow of cherished wood and mediaeval floor tiles, some with the coats of arms of noble families, the Choir lies squarely below the Tower. Above, fanning out from each corner in exquisite traceries of colour is the painted lantern ceiling, part mediaeval and part with added Episcopal coats of arms dating from 19th century restorations. It is enclosed by a rare parclose screen at its eastern end. The choir stalls are carved and painted with the titles of those who sit there. On one is the Royal Coat of Arms, St Davids being the only cathedral to have a reigning Sovereign as a member of its Chapter. Misericords, tip-up seats designed to relieve legs weary of long standing, bear carvings on the underneath sometimes showing the wry humour of a cartoonist with figures suffering from sciatica or seasickness.

The Bishop's Throne was moved into its position on the south side of the Choir early in the 16th century and a central vaulted passageway leads back through the rood screen into the Nave.

Beyond the Choir are the Presbytery, again with a glorious painted roof, and the High Altar. On the northern wall is the shrine of St David where the saint's relics were preserved. The brass plate surmounting the

tomb of Edmund Tudor, father of Henry VII, is a Victorian replica of the original, torn off by rampaging Parliamentary soldiers in 1648.

Henry Vaughan, Bishop, 1509-22, constructed the Holy Trinity Chapel in which he is buried. Fan vaulting in the roof, fine carvings and an altar composed of mediaeval fragments make this chapel particularly beautiful. A nîche in the original external wall holds an oak casket in which bones are kept, at one time thought to be

those of St David.

St Nicholas is not only the patron saint of children but also that of seafarers so it is appropriate that the small chapel at the end of the north Chapel Aisle is dedicated to him.

In the early 14th century the Lady Chapel was added on to the east end of the Cathedral. Its original five bays were later reduced to two and the tombs installed. However, in 1648, the chapel was vandalized by Parliamentary soldiers who stripped the roof of its lead. The building remained open to the elements for over two hundred years. In the early 20th century the chapel was reconstructed at last and the detailed

The Nave of the Cathedral (Above)

carvings of the tombs restored. Several of the original bosses were re-used in the vaulted ceiling. Light, especially in the morning, streams in through elegant windows of stained glass which replace those destroyed earlier.

At this point, indicating the past shift in its foundations, the level of the Cathedral floor before the altar in the Lady Chapel is fourteen feet above that below the West Door.

At the east end of the South Chapel aisle is St Edwards Chapel which has an alabaster altar. In front of this are the Greek letters, Alpha and Omega - 'the beginning and the end'. The tomb is that of Lady Maidstone who donated funds for this chapel and the restoration of the aisle. A display case contains the robes of Bishop Jenkinson, her grandfather, as worn in the 1837 Coronation.

Further along, in the South Transept, hangs a Cretan icon showing Elijah being fed by ravens. The 'Jerusalem Altar' is believed to be the portable altar brought from Jerusalem by St David.

Cathedral & Porth y Tŵr from Quickwell (Above)

The Bishop's Palace

In a wooded valley below the city of St Davids the little river Alun potters amiably towards Porthclais harbour. On either side of its banks stand the magnificent buildings of the Cathedral and the Bishop's Palace.

It is not certain, exactly, when the construction of the Bishop's Palace began. What is known, however, is that due to the political and religious significance of St Davids in the Middle Ages, the bishops appointed to the diocese were men of distinguished standing and some were innovative builders.

Bishop Thomas Bek (1280-93), churchman and statesman, improved on Episcopal properties in St Davids and elsewhere in his see, but it was not until the appointment of Bishop Henry de Gower (1328-47) that the Bishop's Palace was built. Pilgrimages to the shrine of St David were then at their peak; the whole area was important as part of a thriving trade route and considerable wealth was enjoyed.

This period of affluence was destined not to last. The changes brought about by the Reformation resulted in a decline in the income of the church and by the middle of the 16th century the upkeep of the Palace was no longer feasible. By, or supposedly during, the episcopate of Bishop William Barlow (1536-48) the roofs of the halls and state apartments were demolished and the lead from them used for other purposes. The Palace fell into gradual disrepair and only the skeleton of its past glory remains.

Seen from the outside the first and lasting

Bishop's Palace (Above)

impressions are of its architecture, its size and its grace. Constructed around a quadrangle, two sides of the square comprise halls and chapels and their attendant domestic premises built in three phases during de Gower's episcopate. The decoration of façades and parapets with chequerboard arcading is so skilful that, despite differences in building techniques, the main blocks to the east and south appear to be unified. The third range, on the western side, is badly ruined: only some under-floor vaulting remains. A high wall, containing the entry gateway under a stone arch leading into the courtyard, completes the quadrangle.

The bishop's principal living quarters are at first floor level and rest upon vaulted undercrofts or basements. A central porch consists of rising steps leading to a platform from which a passage runs to the Great Hall. Further ahead, the doorway opens into the southern end of the Bishops Hall. Around this substantial hall a series of corbels (carved heads) project at ceiling height. Two curving stairways are recessed into corner walls, one descending and another leading to the parapet wall walk. A now non-existent extension was reached from a doorway opposite the entrance and a second lead into the Bishop's Solar. The fireplace chimney, as seen in old 19th century photographs, was decorated in de Gowers chequerboard style.

The Bishop's Solar (a retirement room) and private apartments lie behind the cross wall. A doorway leads into the projecting east wing probably containing further accommodation and latrines emptying into the river. Decorative corbels adorn the roof line, others, even more ornate, embellish the Bishops Chapel which lie east to west beside the gateway. Here a large window threw light over an alter set against the eastern wall and a blocked doorway once led into chambers over the main gate.

At the other end of the Bishops Hall is the kitchen that must have been a masterpiece of practical ingenuity in its time. It was designed to prepare food for guests in both halls and is linked to them by an added passageway into which two doors open, now barred off for safety. The kitchen was divided into four sections by cross walls meeting at a massive central pillar. Each had an almost conical fire hood over a cooking hearth below. Smoke fed into two pairs of chimneys, north and south. If, as it seems, the ultimate aim in the construction of the Great Hall and the Great Chamber was not only to entertain visitors but also to impress them, then this purpose was achieved magnificently. Leading up to the Great Hall is a wide and stately porch crowned by carved stonework in Caerbwdi Sandstone. The Great Hall is vast, twenty-seven metres to the cross wall. It may have had a rafter roof and walls of decorated plaster. A wooden partition, possibly supporting a gallery, would have screened the busy entrances of the porch, the kitchen and the two corner stairways from guests feasting at the high table opposite. The hall appears to have been heated by central stoves with smoke escaping through vents in the roof.

The crowing glory of the Great Hall is the beautiful and still almost intact wheel window set in the eastern gable.

The Great Chamber, divided from the hall by a wall identifiable by its foundations only, was a stateroom probably used as a withdrawing room. The two doors lead to a latrine extension projecting into the former garden and to the Great Chapel through a 'skew' doorway.

The Great Chapel is partly built into the ruined west range, the east end having a splendid window of three lights beneath which an altar must have stood. An elaborate piscina (a ceremonial hand-washing basin) is built into the wall beside it. Two bells hung in the spire above the west wall and the courtyard steps were porch-covered.

The western block, possibly dating from the 13th century, may have been a ground level hall or stables.

St Davids

Circles, Crosses and a Triangular Square

St Davids is the smallest city in Britain. Here, where the centuries merge over past and present, this old pilgrims' town welcomes all who come to share its mellow antiquity. Cross Square, really a triangle, is the hub of the city. Once a market place, fairground and public meeting place, it is still dominated by the tall mediaeval preaching cross at its centre. This is the remaining one of four, which were in the locality, and was restored and mounted on its stepped plinth of ancient stones in 1873. The Memorial Garden below is laid out in the symbolic form of a Celtic cross with its paths intersecting within a circular wall. The flagpole commemorates three crewmen of the lifeboat 'Gem', lost on the Bitches in Ramsey Sound in 1910.

Photographs taken a hundred years ago show the buildings around Cross Square to be much the same as they are today, but there is no central paved area, only muddy streets. The houses themselves have little architectural interest except for the cottage at the lowest part of the Square. This is typical of the old vernacular style, low walls, small windows and a grouted roof.

The oldest building is, perhaps, Old Cross Hotel, now converted, set back from the Square. The lifeboat, the 'Augusta' was kept in its garden to be drawn by horses to the most suitable launching place. Rooks colonizing its trees create a furious protest when maroons are fired to summon the rescue services, once for the Coastguards, twice for the lifeboat. The private house below has an interesting porch and what was originally a shop window. The RNLI takes daily readings from the barometer outside Court House.

Four old city streets radiate out from Cross Square: Nun Street towards Fishguard; High Street inland, Goat Street leading downhill to the harbours of Porthclais and St

Map of St Davids (Above)

Justinian (lifeboat station) and the unique Pebbles to the Cathedral.

The Pebbles or 'Y Popples', leads dramatically down to the Bell Tower and Porth y Twr. Old maps show a row of cottages down each side of the square-cobbled street, its original narrow width seen at its entry to Cross Square. Now opened on one side, the remaining elegant town houses look over the lovely Cathedral valley, farmland and rocky outcrops to the sea.

Nun Street's name is a mystery. There is no record of a nunnery having been here although there are tales of an underground vault and passageway leading to St Mary's College in the Close. Nun Street could once have been named St Non's Street after Non, St David's mother. Shops and restaurants cluster at the Cross Square end of the street. Two large old granaries at the bottom of Goat Street, at one time known variously as Ship Street or Pit Street, indicate the importance of this road to St Davids during the long period when maritime trade through Porthclais Harbour was thriving. Together with a third big warehouse in Catherine Street, they were used to store not only grain, but also coal and timber, and if old tales are to be believed, smuggled goods.

Apart from a few recent buildings, terraced 19th century houses and shops line High Street. These follow a succession of previous dwellings from the earliest wattle and daub huts to more substantial thatched cottages. All were built along a line of wells and springs, used before the days of mains water. Some may have been communal, but many houses throughout St Davids have traces of blocked wells in their gardens and cellars. At the far end of High Street the National Park's Visitor Centre is above Cocyn Round. This walled grassy mound had to be circled by heavy horse drawn wagons and stagecoaches to enable them to enter the courtyard of Grove House (now hotel) across the road. In turn a vicarage, a school and a coaching house, its walls are built mainly of purple Caerbwdi sandstone reclaimed from the demolished Vicars' College that stood in the Cathedral precincts. Also in High Street are the Police Station, the City and Memorial Halls, built in the 1920s, and the National Trust Centre.

In the mid 19th century there was a custom of limewashing buildings inside and out. Roofs, walls, courtyards, pigsties in front gardens, even parts of the Cathedral were coated. Limewash, used for waterproofing as well as for its cosmetic effect, was readily available from kilns burning culm at Porthclais.

Notes: St Davids Grid Ref OS OL 35 752 254
- ❖ Shops & galleries, petrol stations, post office
- ❖ Restaurants, cafes, pubs, takeaways
- ❖ Hotels, guest houses & B&Bs
- ❖ National Park Visitor Centre(01437) 720392
- ❖ National Trust Centre
- ❖ Ramsey Island boat excursions booking offices
- ❖ Bike hire. Enquire in the Visitor's Centre.
- ❖ Swimming pool at Ysgol Dewi Sant (01437) 721898
- ❖ Oceanarium, Outdoor Activity Centre, Dive Centre, St David's Plant Nursery
- ❖ Shakespearean Plays – Bishop's Palace (during summer) phone (01437) 720517
- ❖ Music Festivals – The Cathedral (Check information centre & book shop) or phone (01437) 720271
- ❖ Car parks: Information Centre (large), Quickwell, & Catholic Church (central) on one-way systems, The Pebbles (limited), Merrivale (near Cathedral) on route to St Justinian.

Lane to St Nons Bay (Above).

New Street, on the one-way system from Fishguard, joins High Street shortly above Cross Square. Tall, pleasant 19th century houses line much of the road. The Post Office was a large shed built to accommodate Coastguard life-saving equipment, housed next to a row of Coastguard Cottages. At New Street's far end, past the Medical Centre, an oceanarium and a children's playground, is what appears to be a railway hotel, built in anticipation of a project which never materialized. In 1870 a grandiose scheme was proposed to connect St Davids to the intended railway from Haverfordwest to Fishguard. A branch line was to join at Heathfield, near Mathry, with a fork to Abermawr, and a station sited between the parallel New Street and Nun Street in St Davids. The hotel was built in advance. Sixty years of problems followed until the project was abandoned in 1930. The suggested station became a bus depot and later the site of a small factory, the St Davids Assemblies which is now in Glasfryn Lane.

Walks around St Davids

Either: ~
1. Walk through the City and Cathedral Close
Or: ~
2. Go Via St Nons.

The route leads through the ancient streets of a bustling, welcoming village - city; along rural footpaths and lanes to wide-open views of a magnificent coast; to the mystique of St Non's and back to the hidden treasures of the Cathedral, its Close and the Bishop's Palace.

Distances: about 2 miles in total, but this can be reduced to a mile for the shorter walk around St Davids only.

Times: allowing for diversions - just over 2 hours for the full walk, 1 hour for walking around the town and Cathedral Close only. Extra time for visiting the Cathedral (1 hour) and the Bishop's Palace (1/2 hour).

Walk One: Through the City

Start by going under the arch of Porth y Tŵr, the old mediaeval Tower Gate at the bottom of The Pebbles. Descend the 39 steps or walk down the road past the Deanery. There is a steep, sharp bend on the corner. Skirt the Cathedral on the Palace side and cross the river over the footbridge. Turn right beyond the Bishop's Palace entrance and continue through the Close to the rest of the route around the City.

Porth y Tŵr (Above), Looking down on Merryvale towards the Deanery (Top Right)

The Cathedral Close

The Close was designed in the form of a circle surrounding a cross, the Celtic Cross. In the 14th century a protective circular wall was completed to enclose the Bishop's Palace, Cathedral and houses of the canons of the Cathedral. Four gateways pierced the wall approximately facing the four points of the compass. Pathways from them intersected centrally at the entrance to the Bishop's Palace, forming a cross.

Only one of the gateways remains intact. This is Porth y Twr, the Tower Gate, facing east towards Cross Square in the centre of St Davids. Its deep old arch abuts onto an octagonal tower built in the 14th century to hold a ring of bells. Perched high on the rim of the valley the peal of the bells can be heard widely over the surrounding countryside. At one time this tower also housed council chambers, reached by ladder, and the town's gaol. Below Porth y Twr the road leads past a steep flight of steps, representing the thirty-nine Articles, descending into the Cathedral churchyard. Further down, the imposing Deanery, rebuilt in the 19th century over the original Precentary site, overlooks a gentle rural scene towards and beyond the Bishop's Palace. A narrow road branches sharply southwest beside the Deanery garden and leads towards Porth Paidrig, St Patrick's Gate. The gap in the ancient crumbling wall is not the true position of the old gate which lay a little below it and was the entrance used by pilgrims coming from the sea through the harbour at Porthclais.

'Chaunter's Orchard' and the fish ponds supplying the kitchens of the Bishop's Palace lay in the field below, where Welsh Black cattle graze the rich grass. This was also the site of the Archdeacon of Carmarthen's house.

The river Alun, bisecting the Close, runs between the Cathedral and the Bishop's Palace and is crossed by a footbridge, and a ford still used by farm vehicles and occasional motorists. There are outlines of windows in the churchyard wall, leading down to the river, where a workshop once stood. Above it was a Chapter house and a school. In 1829 these buildings were removed and the site grassed over. Also in the wall and draining into the river are the openings of conduits carrying redirected water from two wells that once lay behind the Cathedral. Upriver from the ford is Penyffos Bridge connecting the Cathedral with the houses of the Close. '1705' traced in white stones amongst the cobbles dates the pathway outside the Prebendary of St Nicholas with its stone mounting block for horses. Fruit trees once grew in the shelter of the Bishop's Palace and grapes were cropped from green houses. A small rubble-walled building by the bridge, at one time a slaughter house and later a pub named 'The Ship', is now the Cathedral's Visitor Centre supplying books and souvenirs.

Climbing the hill past the Palace a steep, rough track leads to the original site of Porth Gwyn, the White Gate. Now untraceable, it, too, welcomed travellers from the coast. In 1172 Henry II of England

River Alun (Above).

came here from Whitesands to walk in procession with dignitaries of the church into the Cathedral.

At the bottom of the hill, opposite the main gate to the Bishop's Palace, a narrow road leads between the homes of church officials. Older buildings in this part of the Close have been replaced with 18th century and 19th century houses serving the original purposes, their trees casting dappled shade over ancient walls and cobbles.

On the Cathedral side of the road is a wall with battlements enclosing the Treasury garden. Opposite is the Archdeanery, which occupies a site owned by archdeacons since the early 14th century. Next to it is Brecon House where windows in the roadside wall are all that remain of an earlier dwelling. The Treasury itself, again on the Cathedral side of the road, was rebuilt in about

1800. It is believed that St Patrick was born under the arch of an old house in the 6th century and that a stone, still visible in the porter's seat in the wall, was that on which he sat and saw a vision of all Ireland. An alternative to this story claims that he saw this vision from a natural pink-stoned seat overlooking Whitesands Bay.

Beyond the Treasury a lane leads to Cloister Hall, a relatively modern house built over the vaults of the disused St Mary's College to the north of the Cathedral. A fireplace built into the Close wall beyond Cloister Lane is all that remains of the Archdeacon of Cardigan's House. Recent work carried out by CADW[1] has revealed a section of the Close wall here.

The Canonry, formerly the Chancellors house, stands back from the Close road. A large building, in neo-Jacobean style, it also

provides accommodation for the Organist. Its side entrance is over the position of Porth Bonyng of which nothing remains but a newel post. Bonyng's Gate was also known as Bannings Gate for it was here that convicted miscreants were 'banned' or excommunicated before execution outside the Close. This gate was part of the ancient pilgrim route overland from the north.

Outside the perimeter wall the road continues past Wayside and the Bont, once a school, to Pont y Penyd, the Bridge of Penitents, stone-arched over the Alun. Over the bridge the modern road continues up Quickwell Hill, but the ancient Pilgrim's Way follows the wide grassy track northward to meet the coast road coming from Rhos y Brenin. Along this path came pilgrims, bishops and preachers, travel-worn and hungry, on the final stage of their journey to the shrine of St David.

Cross Penitent's Bridge, turning right up Quickwell Hill. Take the left fork past the car park into Nun Street.

The town's gallows stood just beyond the bridge at the bottom of Quickwell Hill, probably so named because of the hooded well which is hidden near the cottages at its top. 'Cwcwll' is the Welsh name for a monk's cowl or hood. Bonws Lane, to the right past the old school canteen, provides a short cut down to the Close.

Cross Nun Street diagonally left up Peter's Lane, identified by a sign reading 'Gallery', into New Street.

Not long ago 'Dai Crust' made wonderful bread at the Grove Bakery, which was almost opposite. After his attendance at a Royal Garden Party his nickname was elevated to 'Dai Upper Crust'.

Choice of route here....
Either: ~ Turn right and walk down New Street into High Street (shops and galleries in both), then return to Cross Square,
Or: ~ Turn left for 50 yards, then right, up a

charming wooded path immediately past the playground, to Glasfryn Lane which leads, to the right, to the main A487 road into St Davids. (Be careful, this short section of Glasfryn Lane is very narrow, no pavements or passing bays). To the right on the A487 is the Visitor Information Centre, and, further down, the High Street returns to Cross Square.

Twˆr-y-Felin, set back, was once a windmill which ceased to grind corn in 1904. It is a landmark well visible from the sea. The road to the nearest beach to St Davids, Caerfai, continues straight ahead from Glasfryn Lane.

Walk Two: The Road to St Nons
Start at Porth y Twˆr, the old mediaeval Tower Gate at the bottom of The Pebbles. Immediately before the arch turn left up part cobbled Tower Hill to Goat Street. Left, and then first right up Mitre Lane. Turn right and bear right off the road, along the bridleway to a T-junction. Go right, then left, opposite the hotel gate, onto the road to St Non's. There is an alternative longer, but very picturesque way, to St Non's Bay. At the bridleway turn left for 200 yards to signposted 'Ffordd Aarron', known locally as 'Foster's Way', which leads around fields to the Coast Path by St Non's. Path can be muddy and slightly overgrown.

St Nons is a place of legend, mystery, religious significance and beauty. Against the magnificent sweep of St Brides Bay, rocky islands and purple cliffs edging the

Chapel of our Lady & St Non (Top),
Ruins of chapel where St David is reputed to have been born (Above)

western sea, is a humble ruined chapel standing on the place where St David is alleged to have been born. A half circle of standing stones shares the Chapel's field with grazing cattle. A cross-inscribed stone leans within the Chapel's Southeast corner. The Chapel is Mediaeval but it may stand on foundations of a pre-Christian era.

St David was born during storms and what may have been a minor earthquake. A spring gushed from the rocks and the well thus formed has been a traditional place of pilgrimage for centuries.

Make a wish at St Non's Well and follow the path around Retreat House to the Chapel of Our Lady and St Non.

This Chapel was built in 1934, modelled on the stonework of Mediaeval chapels around the coast with its altar constructed of stones gathered from ancient sites such as Whitwell priory, once near St Nons Hotel. The piscina came from a chapel at Caerforiog and the holy water stoup is all that remains of the Chapel of the Fathom at Gwrhyd. Stained glass windows depict some of the Saints.

Return towards St Davids but make a detour to Bryn y Garn by turning left along the bridleway past Warpool Court Hotel.

Bryn y Garn, is an outcrop of rock with a wonderful view over the valley of the River Alun to the twin hillocks of Ramsey Island and the sea beyond.

The path around the outcrop is circular - a 10 minute walk. Back to the St Non's road, turn left and go down the hill. Cross the road just after the T-junction, then turn left and follow the high wall down to the entrance to Cathedral Close. Pick up the route through the Close and to the rest of the City from outside the Cathedral.

Cross inscribed stone (Above).

Lone Gull (Above)

Exploring the Peninsula

'With the splendour of late summer
Spread out in the land below me
and stillness where the bare crown
was hewn, the grey outcrop,
and my high fortress looking out over the sea
and the waves once more washing over the rocks'

Waldo Williams (1936)

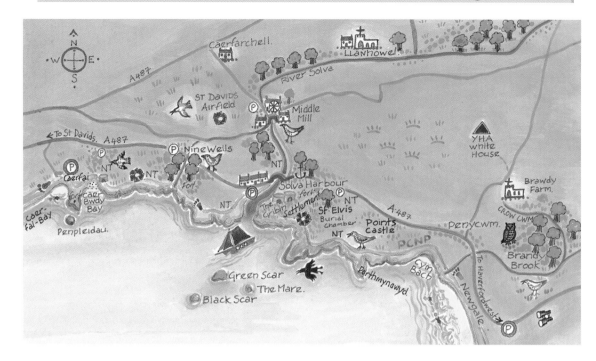

Newgale

Newgale is the largest of the peninsula's beaches. For over two miles soft sand and a vast bank of pebbles, created by the great storm of 1859, stretches hazily into the distance. An old pub once stood on the seaward side of the road until it was eventually washed away by raging winds and tide. More recently, in 1989, yet another violent storm pushed mounds of pebbles across the road, the waves and wind lifted cars into the fields and the buildings along the front were temporarily engulfed by the sea.

Towards the southern end of the beach a chapel marks the place where in 1124 bearers carrying St Caradoc's body to be buried in St David's took shelter from a storm. Having left the Saint's body outside, they emerged to find his body and its covering totally dry.

Traces of quarries marking the western edge of the coalfields that flourished during the 19th century are scattered along the fringes of Newgale.

On the Southern end of the sands there is a walk-through cave. Just beyond the cave, the towering overhanging cliffs are particularly prone to rock fall. At very low tides stumps of submerged forests may appear, which date back to the end of the Ice Age when the land extended much further out to sea.

Meandering Brandy Brook marks the western end of the 'Landsker', a linguistic line dating back to Norman times, dividing the Anglo-Norman of the south from the ancient Welsh of the north.

On the northern end of Newgale and linked to the beach on low tides is the small pebbly

Notes: Newgale Beach, Grid Ref: OS OL 35-850 216
- ❖ Southwest facing, large, sandy beach banked by pebbles
- ❖ Rock pools on the south end but be aware of incoming tides
- ❖ Car parks in middle & both ends
- ❖ Access to the beach at several points with walk over pebbles
- ❖ Swimming, windsurfing, kayaking and surfing, Lifeguards located centrally mid June to Sept
- ❖ Campsite north end, static caravan site south end, a few tourer pitches
- ❖ Cafes, WC (at both ends), pub, garage, surf hire & telephone north end
- ❖ Dog ban on certain parts of the beach between 1st May-30th Sept

Map - Newgale to Caerfai (Above).
St Davids Head from Carn Llidi (Previous Page)

bay of Cwm-bach. The cottage above belonged to the manager of a brickworks which once stood near the cliff edge. A walk up the valley joins Pen-y-cwm.

Located behind Pen-y-cwm, next to Brawdy Farm, is Brawdy church. The original site was dedicated to St Bridget, an Irish saint of the 6th century. The daughter of a pagan chief, Bridget founded both a nunnery and a monastery on the Currach in County Kildare. It is not known if she visited this part of Wales but she was greatly revered by Celtic Christians. St Bridget of Kildare was also known as St Bride and the whole bay is named after her.

Pointz Castle & St Elvis

Further north is Porthmynawyd Bay, an attractive, peaceful cove, protected by what is perhaps one of the most characteristic headlands in Pembrokeshire, Dinas Fach. Its very prominent shape has often been

painted by artists and captured in photographs. The final large rock looks rather like Queen Victoria's face in recline.

A number of small Mesolithic-bronze flints have been discovered on the land surrounding the bay. A mile inland beyond the small valley of willow trees and sea buckthorn, is the site of 12th century Pointz Castle. Only a grassy mound and surrounding ditch remain of the motte and bailey early fort. It was once the Norman castle of a knight and tenant of Peter de Leia, Bishop of St Davids, 1176-1198. Originally, a wooden watchtower would have perched on the flattened mound surrounded by stakes.

Lead and silver were mined for over three and a half centuries at 'St Elvis Lead Mine' on Dinas Fawr, the next main headland. Along the ridge, peregrine, ravens and chough haunt the high cliffs.

Just inland the remains of a Neolithic cromlech with two chambers, once covered in earth, lie on the seaward side of St Elvis Farm.

Within the complex of the farm buildings is the site of St Teilo's Church, the font and cross from which is now housed in St Aiden's Church in Solva. St Teilo was a 6th century bishop and one of St David's

Notes: St Elvis Grid Ref: OS OL 35-817 244
* Cromlech, scenic, coast & woodland walks
* St Elvis can also be approached via the A487 Solva to Haverfordwest. First right one mile from Solva
* Limited parking on National Trust land (1/2 mile walk to coast)
* Walk to St Elvis farm and follow sign posts to the coast

View from Newgale North (Top Left), Porthmynawyd Bay (Above Left), Dinas Fawr (Above Right).

companions, both when he founded his monastery and later on pilgrimage to Jerusalem.

St Elvis was David's religious tutor who was reputed to have foretold the Saint's renown.

Solva

Solva (Solfach), nestling in a dried river valley embracing a sheltered natural harbour, has been described as the loveliest village in North Pembrokeshire. The true origin of its name is unknown; it could be Norse, from the time of the Viking invasions, Sol Vo meaning a sunny fjord.

The harbour was once a busy trading port. Long before the great pilgrim influx to St Davids and throughout the ensuing centuries it was safer and more reliable to transport goods and passengers by sea than by land. Solva's importance grew in the 18th century. Larger than nearby Porthclais, it could accommodate ships of up to three hundred tons. Coastal trading ships tied up at quays discharging cargoes of coal, wood and culm and taking on grain, butter and woven woollen goods destined for Wexford, Bristol and beyond. Supporting this commercial industry and that of local agriculture, Solva's main street was lined

haphazardly by warehouses, mills, smoke-belching lime kilns, stables and carriage houses. Between them were the workshops of tradesmen; blacksmiths, wheelwrights, carpenters, saddlers and weavers. Away from the noise and fumes thatched cottages crept up the curving hillsides and along the little valley towards Middle Mill.

Although it is a safe anchorage the entrance to Solva harbour is both difficult and dangerous. Rocks and hidden reefs, both along the coast and out to sea, caused the loss of ships and lives. In the 1770s ship owners commissioned the first lighthouse to be set up on the Smalls, rocks protruding from the sea twenty-three miles to the south-west. Initially the wooden structure was assembled on the Gwadn and then transported to the Smalls. Basically, a large hut lashed to the rocks by great oak beams and iron stanchions this lighthouse was designed by William Henry Whiteside, a violin maker, and functioned for 86 years. Trinity House bought the Smalls in 1885 in order to build a permanent lighthouse. Granite from Cornwall was dressed and shaped on the improved Trinity Quay and the interlocking blocks shipped out by tug to the assembly site. The resulting Smalls Lighthouse, now automated, is visible on fine days, gleaming pencil-slim to the north side of Grassholm.

By the early 18th century there were thirty ships owned and registered in Solva and sea trade was at its height, soon, however, to suffer a rapid decline. The railway reached Haverfordwest, road transport was mechanized, easier and cheaper, regular boat services ceased and the quays lay

Solva Harbour (Above), Drascomb Lugger (Right).

deserted. But the same improvement in overland transport which brought misfortune to Solva's maritime trade encouraged a steady increase in tourism, now second only to agriculture as a source of employment. Today Solva's tall warehouses and mills are filled with lively little shops, restaurants and pubs. The grimy lime kilns have gone and the harbour yields to the gentle bustle of small yachts, sailing dinghies and fishing boats.

Facing out to sea, Gribin headland lies to the left of Solva estuary. A handful of restored lime kilns perch above high tide

level. Behind them, the Coast Path climbs gently to the highest point. Inland the wooded valley of Solfach River runs back to Middle Mill. A few remnants of a large promontory fort which bestrode the Gribin, with a hundred-foot drop on either side, are just visible in the scrub. Over the harbour, cottages on the hillside, pink washed and creamy white, overlook the quays. Small boats bob at their moorings when the tide is in. Across the river mouth St Elvis Rock and Black Rock both protect and menace the harbour. In 1882 Black Rock was lime-washed white to make it visible and not long ago Solva had its own pilot. Sixty lives were lost in a shipwreck on Black Rock in 1773. Out to sea Black Scar, Green Scar and The Mare jut above frothing waves. Gribin stream runs down the next valley to Gwadn beach. Pebble ridged but safe and sandy at mid and low tides it can be

reached by walking round the point at low water.

Solva had eleven lime kilns along the side of the harbour and within the village. Lime is essential to counteract the slightly acid soil of the St Davids Peninsula, and it was also used for building and to lime-wash houses inside and out. The lime was produced by burning a mixture of anthracite and limestone in kilns and retrieving the residue of pure lime from the hollows below.

Middle Mill

Middle Mill is less than two miles inland up the deep valley. A mill has been in existence here since the 14th century. Still working, but with looms run now by electricity instead of water from the leat, it has been in continuous production since 1907. The original water wheel will be replaced after restoration. The bowl of a disused quarry is scooped from the hillside; some of its obsolete and rickety old buildings remain. A weigh-bridge is near the cross-roads and five arched loading bays face the stream, surrounded in the summer by spires of hot pink rose-bay willow herb.

Directly opposite the Woollen Mill a narrow road signed to Whitchurch turns up the hill following the old main road to St Davids. A pilgrim route from Carmarthen and the way to market in Haverfordwest, it passes the gnarled lichen-covered 13th century church of St David. In Whitchurch, there stood a tall way-marker cross, where pilgrims rested before crossing Fford y Mynach into the sanctuary land

Notes: Solva Harbour Grid Ref: OS OL 35-806 243
- 4 miles southeast of St Davids on A487
- Harbour, quays, boats, fishing trips
- Annual Inshore Regatta (early August)
- Sailing races throughout the summer
- Free Parking at harbour, WC. Foodshop & Post Office, organic walled garden(Upper Solva)
- Shops, galleries, pubs, guesthouses and aquarium
- Lovely walks, swimming at Gwadn beach
- Lime kilns, Iron Age Fort
- Woollen mill (2 miles inland)
- Moorland walks (some suitable for wheelchairs) at old airfield 2 miles inland
- Pottery and Gallery in Caefarchel and Carnhedryn 4 miles inland

Gribin Headland (Above).

around St Davids. In Norman times the parish of Whitchurch included Solva and St Elvis.

St Davids Airfield

Next to Whitchurch, the narrow country road skirts a disused World War Two airfield from which three squadrons of RAF Halifax bombers once patrolled the western sea. Now it is part of an imaginative nature conservancy experiment. Land that was requisitioned is farmed once more and the

Pembrokeshire Coast National Park bought a remaining two hectares in 1996 with aid from the WDA (Welsh Development Agency). The old runways remain but a system of criss-crossing footpaths, banks and bridle-ways pass over an area of moor and grassland, reclaimed wet heath land and heather brush, further skirting existing wet heath land (which has been extended), it is hoped that this improved habitat will increase the numbers of the rare fritillary butterfly and nesting skylarks.

Circular Walk 1

Solva Harbour to Pointz Castle return via Lochvane, St Elvis
Duration: Approx. 8 km / 5 miles
Terrain: Moderate - coast path, fields, inland footpath, woodland & river walk.
Sights Beautiful coastal scenery, harbour, lime kilns, remains of ore & silver quarry, early Norman quarry, burial chamber
Plants Coastal wild flowers, woodland & marsh plants
Birds Ravens, chough, birds of prey

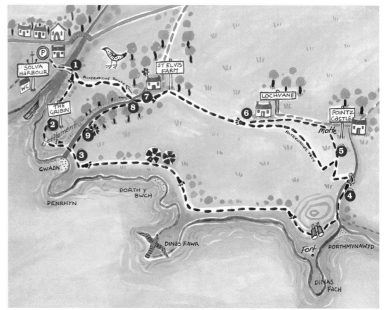

1) From Lower Solva Harbour cross the footbridge over the river & take the footpath indicated almost straight ahead.
2) Keep left up this path until you reach the ridge of the Gribin, carry on towards the sea and follow the steep path on the left that leads down to the beach at Gwadn.
3) Continue up the Coast Path on the other side and cross the fields towards the headland of Dinas Fawr. Carry on to Dinas Fach and Porthmynawd beach (Pointz Castle beach).
4) From the beach take the path that leads inland, on the right is a ruined cottage and then a path to the left and a footbridge which crosses a stream.
5) Follow the field boundary on the right until you come to another field with a gate and a stile on the right. Cross this field keeping to the left edge until a gate is reached, turn left to the lane; at this point on the right is the Mote (the mound of an early Norman castle) at Pointz Castle.

6) Go left, follow the lane through the hamlet of Lochvane bearing slightly left after the last house until a stile appears. Follow this path over several stiles until you reach St Elvis Farm. Just before the farm buildings turn left over the stiles and go right next to the fenced Neolithic Burial Chamber.
7) Carry on along this track until you reach a stile on the right, go over into a field and once over the next stile turn left and take the wooden gate through the woodland.
8) After the woodland take the right fork and go down towards the stream, continue straight ahead (the bridge to the right goes back up to the Gribin and this slightly shorter route can be taken).
9) Continue keeping the stream on your right and follow the path back to the Gwadn and then right back onto the original path over the Gribin to Lower Solva.

Solva to Caerfai

Large oil tankers sometimes shelter in St Bride's Bay, which stretches across the horizon, breathtakingly beautiful. Skomer Island, internationally known as a nature reserve, wallows like a flat backed whale, hazy blue to the south. Alone, isolated and almost straight out to sea lies the singular hump of Grassholm Island. To the north of the Bay, Ynys Bery and the southern end of Ramsey Island may appear to be part of the mainland hidden beyond the Treginnis peninsula. West of Solva the Coast Path marches steadily along cliffs of sandstone and igneous rock, beside inlets and sandy bays, and an ever-changing sea.

On the north-western side of Solva Harbour, opposite the lime kilns, are small quays and jetties where, rigging jangling in the breeze, boats are laid up out of winter-rough water. A weigh-bridge was at the top of Trinity Quay near the one-time Lifeboat and storage sheds and a well still provides untreated drinking water. Climbing steeply past a stone initialled TH (Trinity House) the path turns sharply right, then left, rising to the headland of Pen Craig and spectacular views of the whole sweep of St Brides Bay. Westwards, sometimes easy, at others rough, the Coast Path leads over magnificent cliffs, their formation varying around every corner. There are caves in these cliffs, some of their names betraying past illicit use. Ogof Tobacco (Tobacco Cave) is said to have had a secret tunnel leading up to Llanunwas House. Smuggling was rife and local people became expert wreckers, luring ships onto sharp rocks with moving lights tied to donkeys' tails. Near an old copper mine the 'Smugglers' Steps' are cut into the cliff. Following cliff contours, past jagged rocks and headlands, the path leads to the bays of Aberlong where the hulls of three tugs, wrecked in 1986, were impaled.

Nine Wells Valley, appropriately named, runs down beside Mutton Farm to Porth y Rhaw. Several butterfly species enjoy its shelter and that of irrigation pools harbouring water loving plants such as yellow flag iris, marsh marigold, ragged robin and willow. In the Middle Ages a hospice for the sick stood at Llandruidion. Here, ailing pilgrims were bathed in a holy well before being taken by cart to St Nons to complete their cure and then to a blessing at the Cathedral.

Ogof Castell, an Iron Age Fort, is built on a sheer promontory above Porth y Rhaw. Neolithic flints found on the site suggest that it may also have been occupied before the Iron Age.

Only one wall still remains standing from Porth y Rhaw's once busy wool and corn mills, which ceased working in 1915. The mills were driven by water wheel.

Along the path, in earth-filled stone walls and rock crevices, spread-rooted sea campion, thyme, thrift, trefoils and stonecrop bloom in seasonal tuffets of colour amidst springy turf. The shrill, wild cries of gulls echo between the cliffs.

The mysterious Ffos y Mynach (Monk's Dyke) starts from an inaccessible cave at Ogof y Ffos and runs north for five miles across the St Davids peninsula to end at

Notes: Caerbwdi Bay,
        Grid Ref: OS OL 35-768 249
❖ Small rocky cove, south facing, attractive walk to bay
❖ Caerbwdi Sandstone used in the construction of the Cathedral
❖ Ruins of corn mill & square lime kiln
❖ Small National Trust Parking Area 1/4 mile from the cove
❖ Take A487 from St Davids to Haverfordwest, after 1mile take turning on right. Take care when returning back on to A487

Looking South from Porth y Rhaw (Above).

Carn Penberi. The purpose of the Ffos is unknown, but for much of its length, a ditch and bank construction is obvious. Theories, legend and place names suggest that it may have been a visible boundary separating the sanctuary land around St Davids from the secular country to the east.

Caerbwdi Bay

Passing over a stretch of heath land where parasol mushrooms multiply in early autumn, the Coast Path drops down to Caerbwdi's pebbled beach. On either side, the cliffs are indented with caves and there is another natural arch in the promontory of Penpleidiau, also the site of an imposing 500 BC Iron Age fort. Cliffs guarding Caerbwdi are covered richly with wild flowers, but the main interest lies in their geological formation. From here distinctive purple sandstone was quarried and hauled by cart to build St Davids Cathedral. Part of the quarry was re-opened recently to supply stone for restoration work on the Cathedral. Remains of a mill and a square lime kiln rest in the valley above the beach.

Over the thrift and lichen-covered headland is Caerfai, the nearest beach to St Davids.

Caerfai Bay

Caerfai is a tranquil small family beach, south facing and sheltered in a horseshoe loop of high cliffs. There are ample rock pools and the beach is sandy except at high tide. To the left there are deep caves which may only be accessed at very low tides. On a mid to high tide, when there is heavy swell out to sea, the waves gather enormous momentum and size as they force their way into the narrow bay and crash down onto the shore. The huge swelling backs of the waves, before they break, are a remarkable and mesmerizing sight from the cliff tops.

Some of the purple sandstone excavated from below the car park was used for the building of St Davids Cathedral.

On the stone walled side of the Coast Path lizards sometimes bask spread-eagled, absorbing sunshine warmth. Early summer brings snowflakes of blackthorn blossom, musky gorse, thrift, great clumps of sea campion and ox-eye daisies.

Notes: Caerfai Bay, Grid Ref: OS OL 35-759 245
- ❖ The nearest beach to St Davids 1/2 mile.
- ❖ South facing
- ❖ Rocky, but sandy as the tide recedes with rock pools
- ❖ Popular for swimming and snorkelling
- ❖ The beach is reached by a short but steep path with a few steps at the base
- ❖ Free car park/no amenities
- ❖ Caravan and camp sites
- ❖ Organic farm shop
- ❖ Take the A487 from St Davids to Haverfordwest & turn right just past the National Park Visitor Centre

Caerfai Bay (Above).

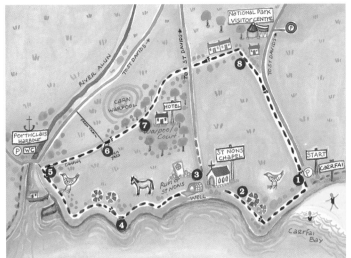

Kilns

Plants Coastal wild flowers, lichens

Birds Fulmars

1) Starting at Caerfai Bay follow the Coast Path towards St Nons Bay.

2) View point.

3) Chapel of Our Lady & St Non, St Nons Well, ruins of St Nons Chapel (in Field).

4) Mad Point (exposed to storms).

5) Porthclais Harbour - as you walk along & above the harbour take a path on your right (fairly difficult to locate) before you descend to the harbour.

6) Go through a caravan/camping field & as you enter the farm courtyard turn left onto lane & immediately right over a stile into a field, keep straight until you reach a narrow footpath.

Circular Walk 2
Caerfai Bay to Porthclais Harbour return by inland path past Carn Warpool.
Duration: Approx. 5 km/3 miles
Terrain: Fairly easy - mostly coast path, field (can get boggy), inland footpath & bridleway, short minor road
Sights Beautiful coastal scenery, ruins of St Nons Chapel, St Nons well, Chapel of our Lady & St Non, Standing Stones, Porthclais harbour & Lime

7) As you reach a wider lane (just off the path to your right is another path which leads to a bench & panoramic viewpoint from Bryn y Garn). However keep straight on the lane keeping Warpool Court Hotel on your right & cross over small lane to a bridleway keep straight ahead & follow this to the end.

8) Keeping right, join the Caerfai Lane back to the bay.

St Nons Bay
(For location see St Davids' map, page 39)

The Coast Path meanders past lichen clad stone walls and a dip to an ambling stream surrounded by horsetail and crossed by stones. At the top of the ridge on the northern side, the views extend across St Nons Bay; here the flower covered cliffs with views onwards to Ramsey Island are lovely. St Nons has some of the earliest spring flowers, thrift, sea campion, violets and

Notes: St Nons Bay , Grid Ref OS OL 35-752 244
- ❖ Peaceful
- ❖ Beautiful cliff top views & walk
- ❖ Ruins of St Nons Chapel, standing stones
- ❖ St Non's Well
- ❖ Chapel of Our Lady & St Non
- ❖ Parking, no amenities
- ❖ St Davids. 1/2 mile

stitchwort. Fulmars nesting on the cliff ledges weave on the wind's updraught, hugging the cliff's contours. The ruins of the Chapel where St David was reputed to have been born lie in the field, the cross inscribed stone which leans in the south-west corner may date from this time. St Non who went to live in Britanny after the birth of her son, is

St Nons Bay (Above)

55

buried in the Chapel of Dirinon in Finisterre. St Non's Well is sheltered above on the path and the Chapel of Our Lady and St Non, built in the 1930's, stands within the grounds of the Passionist Retreat, which was once the summer home of a rich Victorian.

opening difficult to locate from the sea, Porthclais has served as the port of St Davids for centuries. Possibly, Neolithic man in his elementary canoe came through here, certainly invading Vikings and pilgrims on the final stage of their journey. Maritime trade brought prosperity to Porthclais until the early twentieth century. Small shallow-draught trading ships brought coal, culm and wine, reloading with grain, woollen cloth, malt and butter for Bristol and Ireland. The creators of the Cathedral may have built the first harbour wall and quays, when wood was needed, as well as lime for mortar, tools and food. For hundreds of years fishing boats have eased out on one tide, back on the next.

A car park which also acts as a winter storage for boats now replaces the old coal yards and partly hidden by a brick wall, are the remains

Porthclais

Swathes of wild flowers, cliffs thick with the sweet scent of gorse lead on to Porthclais, a safe tidal harbour with several restored lime kilns. Here moored boats are scattered between the creek's sheltered cliffs, a haven for many small birds.

St Elvis Bishop of Munster baptised St David here. During the baptism, water splashed in the eyes of the blind monk, Mori, who was holding the baby and he regained his sight. At the time clear spring water suddenly gushed from the rocks, Ffynnon Dewi, David's Well is now hidden by undergrowth on private land.

In winter, when bared twigs of blackthorn reveal its rocky sides, Porthclais has an aura of primeval existence, which may be why this location was utilized for part of the BBC's adaptation of C.S Lewis 'The Chronicles of Narnia'.

Deeply cut into surrounding cliffs, its

Notes: Porthclais Harbour,
          Grid Ref: OS OL 35-741 243
❖   Picturesque, good walks, lime kilns
❖   Picnic tables by harbour
❖   Free Parking, WC, camping above harbour
❖   Slipway with launching fee
❖   Go down Goat Street from Cross Square, St Davids & follow road round to Porthclais (approx. 1 mile)

Cottage at Porthclais (Top Left), and Harbour (Right).

from the gas works demolished in 1967. Spring daffodils and a summer glut of willow herb colour waste ground, and tendrils of ivy envelop the ruined 'Mariners Arms' at the harbour head. Owned and tended by the National Trust, the harbour wall has been fully restored. With a slipway into the river, Porthclais is ideal for launching sailing dinghies and canoes.

Porthlisgi

Porthlisgi bay, reached over a bracken-strewn path is a quiet shingle beach, often littered with flotsam. It is named after Lysgi an early Irish raider. The ruins of the first St Davids Lifeboat Station, in use between 1869-1888 can be seen close to the track.

Treginnis

The steep path northwards from Porthlisgi rises to the Treginnis peninsula, the westernmost point on mainland Wales. In the central plateau, stone and earth banks separate traditional small fields. The ruins of a copper mine utilized between 1825-90 can be seen at Penmaenmelyn (there is a further filled shaft to the south at Porth Taflod), little evidence exists as to its true productivity. In 1883, a fatality occurred and despite negotiations, it was never seriously put into operation again.

Along this stretch of coast, the mournful call of the grey seal can frequently be heard echoing from rocky inlets and caves. Off the peninsula lies Ramsey Island, separated from the mainland by Ramsey Sound and a series of treacherous spiny rocks known as the 'Bitches'.

On a full flood, the tide races through the sound at around seven knots, and through the Bitches at up to twenty knots, creating a dangerous bubbling water system of rapids and whirlpools. Off the Coast Path to the left, reached by a steep narrow path, stands the old concrete quay of Carnarwig, which once provided shelter and deep anchorage for boats running to Ramsey Island Farm. At the heart of the peninsula stands the National Trust working farm of Lower Treginnis; some of its buildings have been leased to a charity, 'Farms for City Children', providing children contact with rural farming practice. Early farmers of the peninsula recognised the benefits of the stony soil. Known as 'trapland', the stones help to retain both heat and moisture thus enriching the soil.

Towards St Justinian, Castell Heinif is one of the most impressive of the early Iron Age promontory Forts, with a double embankment and deeply excavated ditch. Over this stretch of the coast a profusion of wild flowers, bluebells, campion and thrift create a vivid display of colour.

Map - Porthclais to St Davids Head (Left).

6) Turn inland towards Lower Treginnis Farm (owned by the National Trust) some imaginatively converted outbuildings, dove cote & old farm buildings.

7) Walk through farmyard & follow lane through second farmyard of Upper Treginnis until you reach the road.

8) Follow until you reach a cross-roads bear right & follow road back down to Porthclais harbour.

Ramsey Island

Ramsey Island, lying off the point of the St Davids peninsula, can neither be missed nor ignored. Always imposing, benign in the sunlight, awesome in winter storms or mystically enshrouded in sea fog, Ramsey Island, with its twin hillocks, is seen from long distances on land and from the sea. Sheer cliffs drop into the Atlantic on its western side. Dangerous currents sweep between it and the mainland on the eastern side.

Ramsey's name is Nordic in origin, the Island of Ram, but its Welsh name is Ynys Dewi, David's Island.

The Island, one and three quarter miles long and one wide, can mostly be walked around. Treeless, the vegetation is of gorse and blackthorn, heath and moorland plants,

Circular Walk 3

Porthclais harbour to Treginnis return inland
(The walk can be extended to St Justinian)
Duration: Approx. 8 km/5 miles
Terrain: Moderate - coast path, farm lanes and some minor roads
Sights Spectacular views of Ramsey Sound, wild and rugged, lime kilns, ruins of copper mine. Dove cote & old farm buildings at lower Treginnis. Towards St Justinian: Iron Age Fort, ruins of a chapel, Flemish chimney
Plants Coastal wild flowers
Birds Birds of prey, stonechats etc.
Seals Around Treginnis headland. **Porpoises** In Ramsey Sound. 1) Start at Porthclais Harbour, lime kilns, boats and sheltered harbour. Take the Coast Path to the right.
2) View point across Carreg Fran.
3) Porthlysgi, shingle bay, Lifeboat originally housed here. Carry on up the path (fairly steep) towards the Treginnis peninsula.
4) All around this part of the coast grey seals may be seen & porpoises in Ramsey Sound. Disused mine shaft.
5) Old jetty to the left of footpath once used for Ramsey boats.

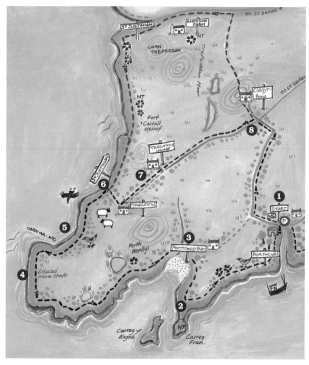

St Justinian (Porthstinian)

If ever a coastline was designed to cause shipwrecks then that of the St Davids peninsula must be it. A hundred major shipwrecks occurred between 1750 and 1950, and they continue. Rescue services, the Coastguards and Lifeboat, with helicopter back-up from RAF Chivenor, stand by awaiting calls for help. The RNLI is part of St Davids' life and there is a waiting list of would-be crewmen. St Justinian, a busy little harbour for pleasure boats,

with once-cultivated fields returning to natural grassland. There is apparently a native conifer, a Juniper (*Juniperus communis*), found on the sides of coves on the east coast of Ramsey.

Although access has always been difficult intrepid farmers tilled Ramsey's plateau fields for centuries, surviving plagues of rats and rabbits and the ravages of salt-laden wind. Sheep, goats, cattle and even deer grazed the grassland while fields of barley and rye thrived in the mild climate to be harvested and shipped across the Sound for milling.

Inevitably, in such a place, true history is irrevocably mixed with legend. There are tales of an isolated monastery containing many human bones, thought to be those of monks; of pirate Vikings hiding behind the islands ready to strike; of a headless Saint; of the Tylwyth Teg, the 'little people' who lived on the coastal islands of Pembrokeshire.

The RSPB now owns the Island protecting the large seabird colonies and grey seals.

Several organized boat trips encircle Ramsey Island and details of these and of landing arrangements are available from information offices in St Davids.

Notes: St Justinian Grid: SM OS OL 35-724 257

- ❖ St Davids Life Boat Station
- ❖ Mediaeval conical Flemish chimney at Rhosson (on left of lane past the chapel heading to St Justinian)
- ❖ Boat excursions to & around Ramsey Island with sea bird colonies & grey seals
- ❖ Good access point to the coast & scenic coastal walks
- ❖ Ruins, St Justinian Chapel
- ❖ Iron Age Fort at Castell Heinif
- ❖ Parking no fee (sometimes full)
- ❖ Go down Goat Street from Cross Square, St Davids & turn sharp right towards the Cathedral and follow signs to St Justinian

Ramsey Island from Coast Path (Top Left), Razorbills (Above).

houses the red-roofed Lifeboat Station, built in 1911-12; its slipway plunges into Ramsey Sound creating dramatic launches.

In 1869, the first lifeboats came to Solva and St Davids. Later, the newly formed Royal Lifeboat Institute amalgamated them and the Solva boat was sold. Having been kept in a garden in St Davids the 'Augusta' was transferred first to Porthlisgi and finally to the present station. There have been several lifeboats since; including the 'Gem' lost on the Bitches in 1910.

From here boat excursions run to and around Ramsey Island, where, depending on the season, the seabird colonies and grey seals can be seen in great numbers.

The now roofless mediaeval chapel dedicated to St Justinian, where little owls have been known to perch, stands above the cove. It was built on the site of the oratory by Bishop of Vaughan of St Davids around 1515, its bells, stolen by the Puritans, were lost in a shipwreck in Ramsey Sound and are now said to chime only during fearsome storms. The Saint's well is to the Southeast.

Circular Walk 4
Whitesands to St Justinian return inland
Duration: Approx. 6 km/4 miles
Terrain: Easy - coast path, farm lanes, bridleway, some minor road
Sights Beaches, Lifeboat Station Folly, Chapel, Flemish chimney, cottages & houses
Plants Coastal wild flowers, pond plants & dragonflies
Birds Kestrel

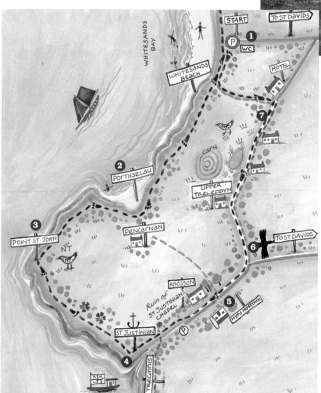

1) From Whitesands walk southwards to Porthselau.
2) Porthselau small sandy beach
3) Tidal races off Point St John
4) St Justinian, Lifeboat Station, ruins of chapel, head inland.
5) Flemish chimney on right
6) Turn left and follow lane through Upper Treleddyn farmyard, bear right onto bridleway.
7) Turn left onto private lane just before Whitesands Bay Hotel, follow right onto footpath & back down to beach.

St Justinian (Top Right), Wild flowers (Above right)

Porthselau

Northwards, the track meanders past fierce racing tides off Point St John and on to Porthselau, a small sandy beach facing northwest with rocky outcrops and pools. Popular with families from a caravan and campsite located in the fields above the beach. There is no immediate parking at Porthselau, so for a day's excursion start at Whitesands and walk south for about 3/4 of a mile, either via the Coast Path or with children along the track marked on Circular Walk 4 from Whitesands.

Whitesands

Whitesands is one of Pembrokeshire's perfect beaches, popular for swimming, surfing and kayaking. As the tide recedes a vast expanse of soft sand is revealed, tinged pale amber between jutting headlands. Beyond, where the sky settles on the horizon, the islands and the flashing of the South Bishop lighthouse stand rigid, and fiery sunsets sweep across the bay floating images at dusk.

On a low tide, on the southern end of the beach is the wreck of the paddle tug the 'Guiding Star'. Its seaweed-clad paddle wheel is exposed on very low spring tides. During the last century the shifting of the sands have revealed the antlers of an auroch, bones of a brown bear and flints which establish a link to earlier ancestors.

A 6th century sailor's chapel, thirteen by thirty feet, dedicated to St Patrick, now marked by a plaque, is located on the grassy bank on the northern end of the bay. It was from Whitesands, in the 6th century, that St Patrick sailed to Ireland in response to a vision commanding him to go. Ty Gwyn, on the hillside below Carn Llidi, stands on the site of a monastery allegedly founded by St Patrick.

Rafts of early blue spring squill carpet the Ram's Nose, a headland protruding into the Atlantic and a good place to watch surfers and kayakers riding the waves.

Whitesands Bay (Above).

Circular Walk 5
Whitesands to St Davids Head, return via Trefelly, YHA & Upper Porthmawr
Duration: Approx. 6 km/4 miles
Terrain: Moderate, coast path, field & farm tracks
Sights St Davids Head Plaque of St Patrick's Chapel, Warriors Dyke, remains of 6 circular hut circles, Coetan Arthur, ancient field systems, Maes-y-Mynedd.
Plants Coastal wild flowers & maritime heathland
Birds Chough, ravens, kestrel, seabird passage at St Davids Head
Cetaceans St Davids Head.
Seals Along coast towards Penberi
1) From Whitesands go right (St Patrick's Chapel, marked by a plaque, left of path), head northwards towards St Davids Head.
2) Viewpoint above Porthmelgan.
3) Porthmelgan sandy on receding tide. Swimming discouraged
4) Remains of Warriors Dyke once 15ft high. Behind foundations, 6 circular huts

5) Viewpoint St Davids Head good for sea-watching
6) Turn & head northwards to Coetan Arthur burial chamber & go right into valley past ancient field systems.
7) Go along the valley (for short cut turn right & skirt around Carn Llidi).
8) Otherwise continue & turn right at first signpost & head inland towards Maes-y-Myndd, remains of

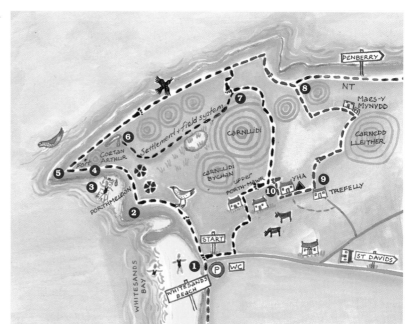

Quaker village now located on your left.
9) Follow path towards Trefelly & just before farm turn sharp right over stile into a field towards YHA.
10) At YHA, turn right back towards Carn Llidi, at gate turn left, follow path and then left to farm and follow lane back down to Whitesands road & to the beach.

Notes: Whitesands Bay, Grid Ref OS OL 35-734 272
❖ Large sandy west facing beach, beautiful views, with access by two slips
❖ Crowded at height of season
❖ Swimming central, surfing & kayaking to the right – dangerous rip current.
❖ Life guards from June-September
❖ Café, ice cream van, surf hire, WC and telephones
❖ Large car park with fee
❖ Dog ban 1st May – 30th September
❖ Access for St Davids Head
❖ Camping & Youth Hostel near beach
❖ Funfair on route to the beach (August)
❖ Just outside St Davids on the A487 to Fishguard turn left onto the B4583 & 1st left again

Gulls on Whitesands (Above).

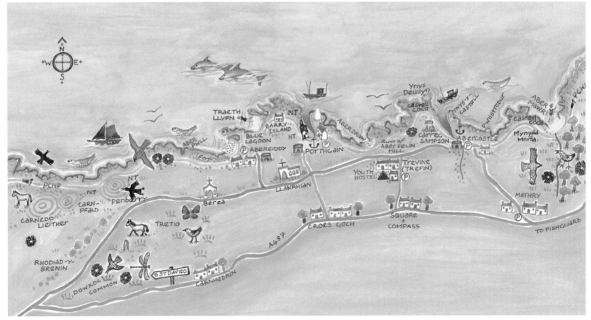

Porthmelgan & St Davids Head

The path to St Davids Head is well worn by the footsteps through time. The salt laden winds buffet the cliffs, where stonecrop and spurrey grow between the cracks in the rocks. From the top of the path leading to Porthmelgan Bay and the maritime heathland of St Davids Head, is the first glimpse of the cromlech Coetan Arthur, perched high on the rock horizon and now wreathed in lichen.

The steep path descends to Porthmelgan, a secluded south-west facing beach with boulders, golden sands and great arched caves at low tide, it's beauty belying the hidden dangerous current and undertow. 'Clawdd-y-milwyr', The 'Warriors Dyke', once a massive fifteen foot high stone wall spans the headland; behind it, traces of six stone hut circles are clearly visible. At the southern end of the wall is Ogof Gafr, Goat's Cave, and at the northern end is the inaccessible Ogof Crisial, Crystal Cave, which was once filled with fine quartzspar referred to as 'St David's Diamonds'.

At St Davids Head it is sometimes possible to catch glimpses of porpoises, dolphins, whales and migrant seabirds.

First excavated in 1898 by Baring Gould, Coetan Arthur is an example of an earthfast, sub-megalithic tomb dating back to about 3,500 BC. A large flat capstone is supported at one end by a single vertical pillar, the other end now rests on the ground.

Between the headland and Carn Llidi the shallow bowl of the valley is hushed. Stone walls of the original small enclosed fields of the Bronze Age Celts, almost 2,000 years old, fragment the landscape between the bracken.

Map - St Davids Head to Abermawr (Top), Porthmelgan (Above).

Carn Llidi

The grassy, rock strewn climb to
the summit of Carn Llidi is
rewarded with arresting views;
buzzards spiral high on warm
wind thermals and chough fly
acrobatically on jagged wings. A
shift in the weather and on a
clear day, the Wicklow Hills of
Ireland appear in the far distance,
while nearer, the mountain peaks
of Snowdonia shine blue in the
clear light. Below, small farms dot
the landscape, with St Davids
Youth Hostel at the foot of Carn
Llidi. To the south St Davids
nestles in the distance.

Between the rocky outcrops of
Carn Llidi and Penberi, below
Carn Lleithr, standing in isolation, are the
ruins of stone cottages dating back to 1750.
Within and beyond the tumbling walls peace
and a quiet solitude prevail. Maes-y-myndd
was a Quaker village, originally six or seven
cottages housing a community of families
until 1832. According to one version a boy,
who unable to walk, was carried on
the shoulders of his two brothers,
to the church at Llanhowell every
Sunday, a round journey of some
12 miles or more. Shrouded in
some mystery, old memories
passed through generations relate
of how the landowner placed a
dead dog in the well, which
contaminated the water and wiped
out the whole community.
Apparently there is no record of
any of the families after this date.

Penberi & Dowrog Common

Penberi marks the northern limit of Ffos-y-
Mynach (Monk's Dyke) although there is
uncertainty as to its exact boundary. One
theory suggests that it ended at the cliffs
edge and another that it ended at a
settlement, which existed where the quarry

now stands. There are extensive views
from the top of Carn Penberi or Kite's
Head Rock, particularly back towards
Carn Llidi and the islands. Inland from
Penberi is Dowrog Common. The old
pilgrim track from Nevern passed through
Rhodiad y Brenin to St Davids and
skirted the Dowrog Common, a low-lying
area of wet moorland one mile inland
from Penberi covering 204 acres.
Historically a princes' gift to pilgrims, it
was known as Tyr y Pererinion, the
Pilgrims' Land. At its northern end,

Carn Llidi (Top), View towards Penberi (Centre), Maes y Mynedd (Above Left).

behind the isolated cottage of Drws Gobaith, (the Doorway of Hope), stands Maen Dewi, an eight foot high standing stone, the largest in the area.

As common land the Dowrog is used to graze horses and cattle. Peat cut from it and carted over supporting wooden beams supplied wages-in-kind for poorer farm workers.

Although smaller than it once was, no longer needing a boat to cross the lake, to St Davids' people the Dowrog is theirs, historically and sentimentally. A suggestion in the mid 19th century that a rail line from Mathry should run across the Dowrog was unhesitatingly rejected by the Parish Council.

The Dowrog, managed now by the Wildlife Trust, West Wales, is a protected Site of Special Scientific Interest (SSSI).

of a slate industry which operated between 1830 and 1904. Quarried from the Blue Lagoon, slate was mined and taken by tramway to Porthgain for export. Mining ceased when the seam became exhausted and the quarry was then deliberately flooded by creating an opening to the sea. Plagued by a typhoid epidemic and then assaulted by a great storm in 1938 the people deserted. There are several theories relating to the tower above the Blue Lagoon; it has been suggested that it is an 18th century 'pharos' tower, a 19th century navigation marker or was even a tea place used by the managers' wives.

Below Penberi there is an Iron Age Fort across the headland at Castell Coch where the spring flowers proliferate. A short steep climb down the Coast Path drops to Aber-pwll, a very small rocky inlet, which separates Careau, another Iron Age Fort.

Abereiddi Bay
A few cottages cluster together behind Abereiddi Bay with its slate coloured sands and rocky shore. The tiny fossil graptolites still in evidence once littered the shale fragments on the beach.

Ruins of shadowy cottages and buildings buffeted by salt laden winds are the remains

Notes: Abereiddi Bay, Grid Ref OS OL 35-797 313
❖　West facing, dark sand with pebbles & rocks
❖　Easy access to the beach with slipway
❖　Care when swimming
❖　Car parking directly above beach
❖　WC, ice-cream van
❖　Access to Blue Lagoon
❖　Ruins of quarrymen's cottages & Lime Kilns
❖　Take the B4583 from St Davids & follow signs to Abereiddi. Plant nursery and sheep dog demonstrations on route (Nr Penberi)

Blue Lagoon (Top Right), Abereiddi Bay (Above).

The Blue Lagoon

The lagoon is still connected to the sea by a small channel and the tide rises up and down several metres. Although it is thought to be about 23 metres deep, there are rumours that no diver has ever reached the bottom. The towering cliffs form an incomplete circle around the water and the ruins of the old buildings. Coloured by minerals continually washed out of the rocks, the water within the lagoon is a rich

aquamarine in sunlight, and slate grey in evening light.

Traeth Llyfn

Traeth Llyfn is a sandy beach tucked between dark high shale cliffs and rock formations running to the sea; reached by steep metal stairs there are rock pools for interest and dramatic views towards the round tower standing on the cliffs of Abereiddi.

An eerie cry can cut across the sound of the swelling ocean as these cliffs are a haunt for the peregrine. During the autumn grey seals breed close by.

Porthgain

A cluster of houses surround the central green of the village of Porthgain, which is scattered with the relics of an industrial age, navigation beacons mark the entrance to the small harbour.

Until the slate industry was established Porthgain was a tiny, insignificant village. Its creek may have sheltered a few small fishing boats at one time but its present harbour is man made. Loading slate quarried from Abereiddi directly on to boats was both difficult and highly dangerous. In the early 19th century, an ingenious conversion of Porthgain's harbour opened a safer and more efficient means of transporting quarried slate overland to waiting ships. A narrow railroad was built for trucks to connect Abereiddi to Porthgain and another along new quays and harbour walls. By constant dredging enough depth was created for larger boats. Abereiddi slate was not of the quality preferred for roofs but was excellent for road stone. Slate waste was used for brick-making; crushers, bins and brick-making sheds, housing for traction engines and cottages for workers were crowded into a dusty space behind the

Notes: Traeth Llfyn Beach,
Grid Ref OS OL 35-803 319
- West facing, sandy with rock pools
- Wonderful views
- Care when swimming
- Watch children on the cliff top
- Steep metal staircase to the sands
- No amenities
- Turn left in Croesgoch off the A487 St Davids to Fishguard & head for Porthgain. Take the track left for Barry Island Hotel carry on through farmyard & several gates (please close) follow to the cliff top car park (sometimes fee during height of season)

Traeth Llyfn (Top), Porthgain Harbour (Centre).

harbour. At the time when marine trade dwindled, the industry at Porthgain provided an alternative to agriculture and paid better; seventy to eighty men at a time were employed in its various facets. The slate industry ceased to be profitable in the 1920s and today only the relics of it remain. Tŷ Mawr, the large machinery shed is almost intact. The brick-making and drying buildings with their tall chimneys have been demolished but most of the ruined storage bins and shutes along the quays still dominate the village.

In 1981, fearful of speculators, residents of Porthgain clubbed together and bought the freehold of their cottages.

Three quarters of a mile inland the church at Llanrhian has a rare decagonal font bearing the arms of Sir Rhys ap Thomas.

industry dominate the small harbour of Porthgain. Refreshments & local art galleries.

5) By the road that leads out of Porthgain go right up footpath to farmyard tracks.

6) Follow farm track & onwards bearing left through fields back down to Abereiddi Bay.

Circular Walk 6
Abereiddi to Porthgain return inland
Duration: Approx. 5 km/3 miles
Terrain: Easy- coast path, farm tracks & field
Sights Coastal, The Blue Lagoon, Ruins of slate industry, disused quarries, lime kiln
Plants Coastal wild flowers
Birds Peregrine
Seals Along the coast around both Abereiddi & Traeth Llyfn

1) From Abereiddi go right & up passed ruins on your left and ascend to Coast Path above The Blue Lagoon (keep well away from cliff edge). Follow footpath northwards.

2) Traeth Llyfn is an unusual sandy beach

3) Carry on along footpath past brick buildings to your left & down to Porthgain.

4) The remnants of a brick & slate

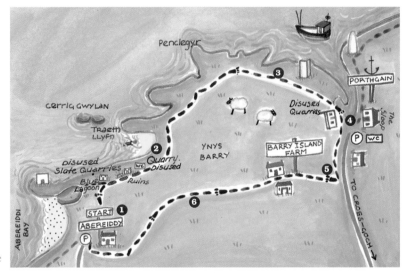

Notes: Porthgain Harbour
       Grid Ref OS OL 35-815 325

❖ Small harbour, lime kiln, derelict brickworks
❖ WC, Boat trips
❖ Galleries, restaurant ,character pub with outside seating, food, children welcome
❖ A487 St Davids to Fishguard, left at Croesgoch, go straight on following sign posts
❖ Gallery in Croesgoch

Trefin
At Aberdraw (known locally as Aberfelin), the closest beach to Trefin, an old ruined corn mill is the 'mill of the manor by the edge of the sea' in Crwys' poem. The 'manor', of the poem, must have been the Palace of the Bishops of St. Davids, who, in Norman times, owned Trefin, the large, cross-shaped village, and all the land around it including

"Mervyn's"shed, Porthgain (Top)

67

Carreg Samson

In the fields at the head of Cwm Badau creek, and reached from the Coast Path, is the megalithic tomb, known as Carreg Samson. It is sixteen feet long and nine feet wide. In a legend Samson trapped and lost his finger while placing the tomb's capstone and, in pain and rage, he threw the dismembered digit across the bay where it landed on Samson's Island at the entrance to the creek of Abercastle. The first Ordnance Survey maps marked the spot with the words "Grave of Samson's Finger".

Longhouse.

Aberdraw faces northwest. The row of small cottages once belonged to the quarry men who worked at Trwyn Llwyd quarry, which stands above the cliffs to the north of the bay. Opened in 1841, it was one of about a hundred in the area, but by 1898 it had closed and the buildings were sold. At the cliff top cattle grazing has been re-introduced in order to encourage a greater diversity of fauna and flora.

Sheer, spectacular cliffs drop from the Coast Path as it edges past coves and rocky inlets, favoured by seals, to the promontory of Pen Castell Coch. The Iron Age Fort was protected by a double earth and stone rampart running across the promontory enclosing a three acre area, its lines clearly identifiable. To the north a natural arch, clearly visible, has been eroded through the rock.

Notes: Trefin , Grid Ref OS OL 35-840 325
❖ Youth Hostel, shop, gallery, weaving centre and courses, pub
❖ Coastal Walks, access to Carreg Samson (across field)
❖ Take the A487 St Davids to Fishguard & turn left in Square And Compass and follow road down to village

Cottages at Aberdraw (Aberfelin), (Top), Natural Arch between Trefin & Abercastle (Above).

Abercastle

Abercastle is an attractive village sheltering in a small valley. In the 19th century it was a busy little port handling imports of anthracite and culm, which were burnt in the large lime kiln at the top of the beach for use on the surrounding rich farmland. Slate was quarried for a time from the cliffs around the village and loaded into outgoing boats, together with corn and butter.

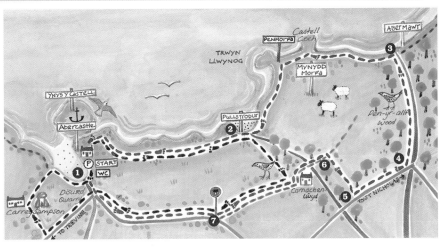

Shipbuilding was unusual locally, but three boats were built here between 1790 and 1820. Two of the harbour-side bollards are converted cannons dating from this time. On the headland is the ruin of an old granary. Northward, a stone wall locally built and nicknamed 'The Great Wall of China' borders the Coast Path part way to Abermawr. The small cove of Pwllstrodur between Abercastle and Abermawr can also be accessed over the fields from the road. Another fort, with a zigzag entrance between its three walls and ditches, stood on Penmorfa, just before Abermawr, dating from about 300 BC.

Notes: Abercastle: Grid Ref: OS OL 35-853 336
* ❖ Picturesque small creek with slipway access
* ❖ Walk to Carreg Samson Cromlech
* ❖ Limited parking, WC
* ❖ Lime kiln
* ❖ Take the A487 from St Davids to Fishguard, turn left at Square And Compass. Follow road & take 1st right hand turning. At T-junction turn right for Abercastle.

Circular Walk 7
Abercastle to Abermawr return inland

Duration: Approx. 8 km/5 miles
Terrain: Moderate - coast path, woodland, farm tracks & minor roads
Sights Picturesque creek, lime kiln, Iron Age Fort, south of Abercastle - Carreg Samson, beach and woodland.
Plants Coastal wild flowers, woodland plants
Birds Fulmars, buzzards, woodland birds

1) From Abercastle take the footpath to the right & head northwards, fulmars nest on Ynys Castell. Path runs along stone wall
2) From Pwllstrodur follow path to Iron Age Fort, Castel Coch & down to Abermawr
3) Head right & enter Pen-yr-Alt woodland; on the other side, either skirt around the field (can get very muddy) or go through field.
4) At the road go through a wooden gateway & turn right. Follow road until you reach first bridleway marked on the right next to a bungalow.
5) Follow along bridleway and at a gate turn left through field, follow to next gateway & turn right onto a farm track.
6) Follow track until it reaches a T-junction & turn left, walk a few metres, track turns into narrow path which dips down to marshy valley & then skirts a farm on the left. At the end, on a narrow farm lane, turn right.
7) Follow lane until you reach the main road, bear right & head back down to Abercastle.
Alternatively, there is another route marked in red which includes Carreg Samson.

Abercastle (Above).

69

Abermawr

Past the undulating inland fields of Mynedd
Morfa and down into a wooded valley is
Abermawr where fossilized stumps of an
ancient forest are seen on very low tides.
Like neighbouring Aberbach it is a recently
formed storm beach; pebbles and shingle
were thrown up in the great storm of 1859.
In the 1840s, Isambard Kingdom Brunel, the
Victorian engineer, contemplated a coastal
terminus at Abermawr to link with a then
proposed Haverfordwest to Fishguard
railroad. The bases of piers to extend into
the sea, north and south, were constructed
at Carreg Golfa and Penmorfa and a track
was laid, just visible now under the trees at
Pen-yr-Allt woodland. However, in 1851 an
alternative site was chosen at Neyland and
the project
was shelved.
Broad-leafed
woodland and
marshland
above the
beaches at
both
Abermawr and
neighbouring
Aberbach,
provide varied
habitats for
wildlife and
many plants.

In 1883, the
first underwater cable message to Ireland
was sent from the cottage on the northern
side of Abermawr.

Fifteen minutes walk following the valley
from Aberbach (North of Abermawr) is a
woollen mill, Melin Tregwynt, which has
been run by the same family since 1912. Its
water wheel still turns although the looms

are now run by electricity. In early spring,
snowdrops whiten the banks around the
Mill.

Mathry

Mathry, two miles inland, was
once a hilltop settlement and fort
commanding the lower ground
surrounding it, from inland valleys
down to the coast. A place of
significance on the old pilgrim
route from the north, the Church
of the Holy Martyrs is dedicated to
seven saints and stands within an
ancient enclosure. The church
porch contains a pillar stone bearing an
inscribed ring-cross on one face and incised
Latin and Ogham lettering on another. Two
more ring-cross stones are inset in the
church wall. As a mediaeval village, built
over the original settlement, Mathry once
had a tradition as a meeting place for great
markets and fairs.

Notes: Abermawr Bay,
　　　　Grid Ref OS OL 35-883 348
❖ North-west facing, secluded beach, sandy as
　the tide recedes, bordered by pebbles with
　woodland
❖ Roadside parking
❖ No amenities
❖ Tregwynt Woollen Mill
❖ One mile northeast of Mathry off the A487
❖ St Davids to Fishguard

Notes: Mathry, Grid ref OS OL 35-879 320
❖ Church, Latin & Ogham Inscription
❖ Pub, shops, including antique shop & wood
　turner
❖ Llangloffan cheese making (2 miles inland)
❖ Outdoor activity centre
❖ Dive centre
❖ Take the A487 St Davids to Fishguard for
　8 miles

Abermawr (Top), Pen-yr-Alt Woodland (Above Centre).

Coast between Abercastle and Abermawr (Above)

Activities

Outdoor Charter

Whether you are walking, cycling, climbing, kayaking, surfing or diving you can still get the most out of the National Park's vast recreation opportunities without damaging the environment. Many local outdoor centres have signed up to the Pembrokeshire Outdoor Charter, and have made a commitment to respecting and preserving the environment.

On Land

Walking

Whatever the season the Peninsula offers forty miles of some of the most scenic coastal walks in Pembrokeshire. Signs depicting a walking figure or a yellow arrow indicate footpaths. An acorn denotes the long-distance trail; bridleways by a ridden horse or blue arrow.

Study the area you intend to walk and choose a suitable route to accommodate your own and children's abilities. In addition to the Ordnance Survey Map (Outdoor Leisure 35) there are 8 illustrated circular walks of varying length and terrain listed in this guide. There are also guided walks and a mini bus tour available within the Peninsula, details from information centres.

Cycling

Cycling is an excellent, eco-friendly way in which to explore the Peninsula, providing you restrict your excursions to roads, designated bike trails, bridleways and tracks. The fairly quiet coastal lanes and a few bridleways and tracks offer some off-road and circular routes. The coastal footpath however is strictly for walking. Details on cycle hire can be obtained from information centres.

Climbing

Early season cliff climbing is exceptional due to the speed with which the cliffs dry out and the rocks warm up. Access and route grades vary, many of which are tide dependent (check climber's guide books and tide tables). Tuition and guides are available from local Outdoor Centres. Some stretches of cliff or specific routes are restricted for climbing during the bird nesting season. Check Information Centre and site notice boards for details, they may change during the season. All climbing restrictions have been agreed by environmental bodies and the British Mountaineering Council.

Coast Path (Top), Climbing at Porthclais (Bottom).

Sailing

The small tidal harbour of Solva provides shelter and a base for day sailing. Tuition is available with Solva Sail Boats during the summer. A few visitors' moorings and launching facilities exist here and at Porthclais, Porthgain and Abercastle. Solva has an annual regatta and is also a venue for highly competitive longboat racing with teams competing nationally.

Sea

Kayaking

Sea kayaking has exploded in popularity around the peninsula. A myriad of inaccessible storm beaches, caves and rock arches create a beautiful and exciting landscape for exploration. Grey seals can be seen year round, they are highly inquisitive, playful creatures and will often follow your boat if not threatened or distressed. However during late summer and autumn particular care has to be taken not to disturb seals while hauled-out on beaches or in caves where they breed. Kayak instruction and day trips are available at St Davids and Mathry Outdoor Activity Centres

Diving

Abundant marine life flourishes in the warm waters of the Gulf Stream and with about 160 wrecks and regular, good visibility, the Peninsula is popular to many UK divers. Boat launching is informal and inexpensive at the harbours (see sailing).

Surfing

Warm Gulf Stream water and Atlantic swells combine to produce good surfing conditions. For the beginner and boogie boarder, Newgale and Whitesands provide reasonable beach breaks, with seasonal lifeguards, equipment hire and outdoor activity centre instruction. Other surf spots can be found around the coast, including Abereiddi and Abermawr depending on the surfers' experience, swell and wind conditions.

Kayaking (Top), Surfing (Centre), Surf at Whitesands (Below).

Boats can also be launched from the slip at Whitesands. Two dive schools at St Davids and Mathry offer charter instruction and hire equipment.

There is a recognised Diving Code of Practice, designed to protect seabirds, seals and underwater life. Sensitive nature conservation areas adjacent to popular dive sites are at Ramsey (west and southeast sides), North Bishop and Careg Rhoson:-
Seabirds at Ramsey (1 March – 31 July).
Seals between St Davids Head and Porthgain (1 Sept. – 31 Dec.)

Whitesands (above)

Directory

References

ANDERSON, Sheila., Seals
(Whittet Books Ltd, London, 1990)

BARRETT, John H., The Pembrokeshire Coast
Path *(Her Majesty's Stationery Office, 1974)*

BOWEN, E.G., The Settlements of the Celtic
Saints in Wales
(University of Wales Press, Cardiff, 1954).

BROOM, Trevor., A History Of Solva
(Trevor Broom, Bristol, 1995)

DARK, K. R., The Inscribed Stones Of Dyfed
(Gomer Press, Llandysul, 1992)

DAVIES, Peter B. S., Dewisland Limekilns
(Merrivale, St Davids, 1989)

DAVIES, Peter B. S., The Footsteps Of Our
Fathers *(Merrivale, St Davids, 1994)*

DONOVAN, Jack., REES, Graham., Birds of
Pembrokeshire *(Dyfed Wildlife Trust, 1994)*

EVANS, Wyn J., St Davids Cathedral
(Pitkin Pictorials, 1991)

FITZGERALD, Michael/KNAPP-FISHER, John.,
Pembrokeshire Churches
(Rosedale Publications, Newport, Pembs., 1989)

FRASER, Maxwell., Introducing West Wales
(Methuen & Co., London, 1956)

GEORGE, Babara, J., Pembrokeshire Sea-Trading
Before 1900 *(FSC publication H2 reprinted from
Field Studies Vol. 2. No 1, 1964)*

GEORGE, T. Neville., British Regional Geology
South Wales
(Her Majesty's Stationary Office, 1970)

GIRALDUS CAMBRENSIS., The Itinerary through
Wales; and Description of Wales *(Everyman).*

GRUFYDD, Dyfed Elis., Rocks and Scenery Of The
Pembrokeshire Coast *(Pembrokeshire Coast
National Park Authority, 1993)*

HAMPSON, Desmond G., and MIDDLETON,
George W., The Story of the St Davids Lifeboats
(Pembrokeshire, 1974)

HOWELLS, B.E. and K.A. (ed), Pembrokeshire Life
1572 -1843 *(Pembrokeshire Record Society, 1972)*

JAMES, David W., St Davids and Dewisland,
A Social History
(University of Wales Press, Cardiff, 1981)

JAMES, David W., Twice to St David's
(Gomer Press, Llandysul, 1995)

JAMES, J.W., Rhygyfarch's Life of St David
(University of Wales Press, Cardiff, 1983)

JONES, Gwyn., JONES, Thomas., (translation)
The Mabinogion *(Everymans Library, 1974)*

JOHN, Brian, S., The Geology Of Pembrokeshire
(Pembrokeshire Handbooks, 1979)

JOHN, Brian, S., Pembrokeshire Coast Path,
National Trail Guide
(Aurum Press Ltd, London, 1990)

LEATHAM, Diana., The Story of St David of Wales
(Garraway, London, 1952)

MARRIOT, H., St Davids Cathedral
(Pitkin Pictorials, London, 1968)

MIDDLETON, G.W., St Davids
(St Davids Civic Society, 1977)

MILES, Dillwyn (ed.) Pembrokeshire Coast,
National Park Guide No 10.,
(Her Majesty's Stationery Office, London, 1973)

MILLER, David., Seals
(Colin Baxter Photography Ltd, Scotland 1991)

O'MALLEY, Brendan., St Davids, Pilgrim Guide
(Cantebury Press, 1997)

RALEGH RADFORD, C. A., The Bishop's Palace
Pembrokeshire
(Her Majesty's Stationary Office, London, 1953)

RAGGETT, Paul., Solva-An Introduction To Village
Life And Guide To The Walks
(Paul Raggett, Solva, 1992)

REES, Nona., St David of Dewisland
(Gomer Press, Llandysul, 1992)

RICH, Lawrence, GARNETT, Oliver., The
Pembrokeshire Coast *(The National Trust, 1996)*

SAMPSON, Alwyin., St David's
(Yr Oriel Fach Press, St Davids, 1974)

SEYMOUR, John., About Pembrokeshire (T.J.
Whalley & Associates, Haverfordwest, 1971)

SHARKEY, John., Pilgrims Way-The Grand
Pilgrimage To St Davids
(Ancient Landscapes, Cardigan, 1994)

WARREN, T.A., DAVIS., F.L.S,. Plants of
Pembrokeshire *(West Wales Naturalist Trust,1970)*

WILLIAMS, Herbert., The Pembrokeshire Coast
National Park, Countryside Commission Official
Guide *(Webb and Bower Ltd, Exeter, 1987)*

WILLIAMS, Paul., Circular Walks In North
Pembrokeshire *(Gwasg Carreg Gwalch, Dyffryn
Conwy, Wales, 1997)*

General Index

W

Waldo Williams, 10, 15, 21, 28, 37, 47
Walking, **72**
Whales, 16, **18**, 63
Whitchurch, 51, 52
Whitesands, 12, 13, 15, 17, 22, 23, 27, 60, **61**, 62, 73
Wild Flowers, **16-17**
Wildlife Trust, The, 16, 65
Woollen Mill, 51, 70

Y

Y Popples, 40
Youth Hostel, 62, 64, 68
Ynys Bery, 17, 53

Maps & Walks

List of 100 photographs

List of 100 photographs

Jacki Sime is a freelance photographer and writer with an MSc in Marine Environmental Protection. Involvement in expeditions and natural history television documentaries in the U.K. and further afield has taken her from rainforests to the Arctic. In addition to running her own photographic agency, Jacki lectures in Planning and Environmental Impact.

Visitor Centre

National Park Visitor Centre
The Grove
St Davids, SA62 6NW
Tel: 01437-720392

Sponsors

Caerfai Caravan Park
Caerfai, St Davids
Haverfordwest
Pembrokshire
Tel: 01437-720274

Pebbles Yard
Coffee Bar, Shop and Gallery
The Pebbles
Cross Square
St David's SA62 6SL

Quality Cottages
Cerbid, Solva
Haverfordwest
Pembrokshire SA62 6YE
Tel: 0348-837874

Voyages of Discovery
1 High Street
St Davids
Tel: 01437-720285
Fax 01437-721911
e-mail:voyofdisc@aol.com

Warpool Court Hotel
St Davids SA62 6BN
Tel: 01437-720300
Fax: 01437-720676
e-mail: Warpool@enterprise.net